MIRAGE III
VS
MiG-21
Six Day War 1967

SHLOMO ALONI

First published in Great Britain in 2010 by Osprey Publishing,
PO Box 883, Oxford, OX1 9PL, UK
PO Box 3985, New York, NY 10185-3985, USA
Email: info@ospreypublishing.com

Osprey Publishing, part of Bloomsbury Publishing Plc

Transferred to digital print on demand 2015.

First published 2010
1st impression 2010

Printed and bound by Cadmus Communications, USA

A CIP catalogue record for this book is available from the
British Library.

ISBN: 978 1 84603 947 8
PDF e-book ISBN: 978 1 84603 948 5

Edited by Tony Holmes
Cockpit, gunsight, three-view and armament artwork by Jim
Laurier
Cover artwork and battlescene by Gareth Hector
Page layout by Ken Vail Graphic Design, Cambridge, UK
Index by Alan Thatcher
Typeset in ITC Conduit and Adobe Garamond
Maps by Bounford.com
Originated by PDQ Digital Media Solutions, Suffolk, UK

Acknowledgements

The author wishes to express his gratitude to both Shahak
pilots and maintainers, friends and colleagues who have
contributed to the production of this volume. Special thanks to
Ezra Aharon, Giora Epstein, Itamar Neuner, Guri Palter,
Avraham Salmon and Jonathan Shahar for fine-tuning the end
product. Thank you also to Asher Roth, Yehuda Borovik, Yoav
Efrati, David Nicolle, Tom Cooper, Lon Nordeen and Raanan
Weiss for their ongoing support, to Doron Avi-Ad of the IDF
Archive and to the Israeli Censorship who approved the
contents of this title for publication. Thanks also to Six Day
War Shahak pilots Yoram Agmon, Ezra Aharon, Amos Amir,
Yossi Arazi, Dror Avneri, Adi Benaya, Gidon Dror, Giora
Epstein, Giora Furman, Ilan Gonen, Reuven Har'el, Eelan
Hight, David Ivry, Yehuda Koren, Uri Liss, Yuval Ne'eman,
Ithamar Neuner, Avi Oren, Eldad Palter, Guri Palter, David
Porat, Giora Romm, Ran Ronen, Reuven Rozen, Avraham
Salmon, Dan Sever, Danny Shapira, Pessach Shraga, Amichai
Shmueli, Menachem Shmul and Avner Slapak for enlightening
the author on aerial engagements during the Middle East's air
wars. Many thanks also to pilots and friends for sharing their
personal memorabilia, especially photographs, for inclusion in
this book.

To save space, as well as to avoid confusion and repetition, no
ranks are mentioned in the text.

Mirage IIIC cover art

Emergency Posting pilot Yoram Agmon of No. 101 Sqn made
history on July 14, 1966 when, during a border clash with the
Syrian Air Force (SyAAF), he became the first Israeli Defence
Force/Air Force (IDF/AF) Mirage IIICJ (Shahak) pilot to claim a
MiG-21 destroyed. Flying as No 4 in a four-ship Combat Air
Patrol (CAP) formation that was tasked with defending Israeli
attack aircraft striking targets on the Syrian border, Agmon's
squadron intercepted a pair of MiG-21s low over the Yarmouk
Gorge – his victim was probably the wingman in the SyAAF
section. The fact that the No 4 man in the Mirage IIICJ
formation was the first pilot to attack reveals the flexibility of
standard IDF/AF tactics when it came to air combat
manoeuvring. The drill was that the first pilot to spot the
enemy automatically assumed the lead position in the
engagement, regardless of his seniority or position in the
formation. Both Yoram Agmon and his aircraft (Shahak 59)
went on to achieve ace status, the former retiring from IDF/AF
service as a brigadier general with six kills to his name and the
latter eventually being sold to Argentina after it had been
credited with 13 victories. (Cover artwork by Gareth Hector)

MiG-21FL cover art

Egyptian Air Force (EAF) fighter pilot Nabil Shoukry and his
section leader were flying an air-to-ground mission over
northern Sinai on June 8, 1967 when they were engaged by a
pair of IDF/AF Mirage IIICJs from No. 119 Sqn. Minutes earlier,
the latter machines had been vectored from their CAP station
onto other EAF jets that had been detected nearby. The Israeli
delta fighters had duly shot down an EAF Il-28 bomber that
was attacking IDF troops, its demise being credited to future
ace Menachem Shmul. Having now spotted the MiG-21s, the
Mirage IIICJ pilots and their EAF counterparts commenced a
classic two-versus-two dogfight. Shoukry subsequently
recalled, "After we had flown over the Suez Canal we spotted
two Mirages heading towards us from the left, so I put the
afterburner on, jettisoned the belly tank and saw that they
were going to attack. I told my leader 'There's a Mirage behind
you'. He reversed, but at that moment his MiG-21 exploded
after being hit by cannon fire. The Mirage then headed towards
el-Arish. I put the nose down and selected maximum
afterburner, but my fighter was equipped with two rocket pods
– my only weaponry – which created a lot of drag. I reached
the same altitude as the Mirage and got to within a mile of it,
but I had no way of closing because it was accelerating. I
started firing unguided rockets at him from each of the pods,
but they fell well short." Three days earlier, however, Shoukry
had succeeded in downing the Shahak flown by Yair Neuman,
which was the only Mirage IIICJ that the IDF/AF admitted had
been downed by an EAF MiG-21 in the Six Day War. (Cover
artwork by Gareth Hector)

The Woodland Trust

www.ospreypublishing.com

CONTENTS

INTRODUCTION

On November 29, 1947 United Nations' Resolution 181 called for the partition of British Mandate Palestine into two states, with one occupied by Arabs and the other by Jewish settlers. Israel's independence was duly announced following the expiry of the British Mandate on May 14, 1948. The next day, the invasion of the Jewish state by the Arab League transformed what had been a conflict restricted to Palestine into a regional war. Fighting continued until early 1949, when the Israeli War for Independence ended in a series of four bilateral ceasefire agreements between Israel and the four Arab League nations sharing a border with the new Jewish State – Egypt, Jordan, Lebanon and Syria.

Hostilities between Arabs and Israelis continued to flare up over the next three decades, however, with Arab nations (especially Egypt under the leadership of President Gamal Abdel El Nasser) adopting an aggressive policy aimed at provoking another full scale war that would eliminate the disgrace of the 1948–49 defeat at the hands of the Israeli Defence Force (IDF).

Such a conflict was certainly not an Israeli objective, but Arab rhetoric was treated seriously nevertheless. Should military action be required, Israel's first Prime Minister, and Minister of Defence, David Ben-Gurion favoured three basic principles when it came to war. Conflicts had to be brief, fought on enemy soil and result in a decisive victory. Such strategies were shaped by the fact that Israel's fledgling economy and small population could not sustain a lengthy war, its territory had no "strategic depth" to withstand fighting and an overwhelmingly decisive victory was required so as to deter Israel's enemies from pursuing all out war for a third time.

The expected Arab "second round" offensive never materialised. The war that followed the 1948–49 conflict came as a result of the Suez Crisis of late 1956, when Israel joined an Anglo-French coalition that attacked Egypt. The Anglo-French objective was to retake the Suez Canal that President Nasser had nationalised. The canal remained in Egyptian hands, however, although all Israeli objectives were achieved – the Egyptian aerial and maritime blockade of the Red Sea was lifted, Egyptian support for Palestinian terror activity in the Jewish homeland faded and Egypt's military option for a viable "second round" war suffered a temporary setback. The Sinai Desert area between Israel and Egypt was demilitarised following the war and occupied by the United Nations Emergency Force (UNEF), which created a buffer zone between the two countries.

The Suez War also saw hostilities in the Middle East transform into a Cold War regional conflict. The Soviet Union dramatically increased its military patronage of Egypt and Syria after 1956, while France was Israel's principal arms supplier during this period. The British and US governments, meanwhile, strived to maintain some influence in the region by supporting "moderate" Arab regimes such as Jordan and Iraq. While politicians in the East and the West struggled to gain the upper hand in their influence of Arab nations during this phase of the Cold War, the most obvious characteristic of the Middle East conflict from a military standpoint was the fielding of Communist weaponry and tactics against their Western counterparts.

Egypt and Syria announced a political union in February 1958 that became known as the United Arab Republic (UAR). While things remained relatively quiet at this time on the Egyptian-Israeli border, armed clashes grew in their intensity along much of the Israeli-Syrian border. The popularity of President Nasser also soared thanks to his hard line rhetoric against the West, and Israel in particular, but clashes between Israel and Syria threatened to shatter his hoped for "Arab solidarity". Finally, Egypt could no longer restrain itself. A series of armed clashes both along and over the Israeli-Syrian border during early February 1960, coupled with the receipt of a Soviet intelligence report that claimed Israel was planning to attack Syria on February 22, 1960 (the date of the second anniversary of the founding of the UAR), forced Egypt into action. Nasser secretly ordered his ground forces into Sinai.

Contrary to the Soviet report, the IDF had no plans to attack Syria, but to the Israeli government the Egyptian deployment resembled the "second round" scenario that it had long feared. Israel in turn quickly amassed regular units and mobilised its reserves in order to face Egypt. Intense diplomatic negotiations led by the West had calmed the adversaries down by March 1960, but their efforts only postponed the war until June 1967 – a delay that ultimately led to a series of one-sided clashes between Arab MiG-21s and Israeli Mirage IIICJs.

CHRONOLOGY

1955

February 14 MiG test pilot Gheorgiy Mosolov flies Ye-2 prototype, first in a series leading to MiG-21.

June 16 MiG test pilot Gheorgiy Sedov flies Ye-4, a Ye-2 with delta wings.

June 25 Dassault test pilot Roland Glavany flies MD 550 Mystere-Delta, a prototype delta-winged light interceptor that was renamed Mirage I in 1956.

1956

January 9 LII Flight Research Institute pilot Valentin Mookhin flies Ye-50, a Ye-2 with rocket-boosted engine. MiG test pilot Vladimir Nefyodov also flies Ye-5, representative of MiG-21 prototype.

November 17 Dassault test pilot Roland Glavany flies Mirage III 001 prototype.

From 1964 through to late 1967, the IDF/AF exclusively flew five French-made combat aircraft types, as seen here during an IDF/AF display. They are, from left to right, the Sud Aviation Vautour, Dassault Mirage IIICJ, Dassault Super-Mystere B 2, Dassault Mystere IVA and Dassault MD 450B Ouragan. By June 5, 1967, the 65 Mirage IIICJs accounted for 32 percent of the IDF/AF fighter force, which totalled 203 combat aircraft.

1958

May 12 Dassault test pilot Roland Glavany flies Mirage IIIA01 first pre-production aircraft.

May 20 MiG test pilot Vladimir Nefyodov flies Ye-6, pre-production MiG-21.

October 24 Mirage IIIA01 becomes first Western Europe aircraft to fly faster than twice the speed of sound (without booster rocket) when Dassault test pilot Roland Glavany passes Mach 2.

1959

June 23 IDF/AF test pilot Danny Shapira flies Mirage III, becoming first Israeli to fly in Mach 2 fighter.

1960

March MiG-21F becomes first production model to enter squadron service with Soviet Air Force.

May Israel orders 24 Mirage IIICJs, with option covering 36 additional aircraft.

October 10 Dassault test pilot Jean Coureau flies first Mirage IIIC interceptor version.

1961

April 28 Israel converts 24 Mirage IIICJ option into firm order.

| July 7 | Europe's first operational Mach 2 aircraft is a Mirage IIIC delivered to *Armeé de l'Air*. |
| September | Israel places third Mirage IIICJ order covering 24 additional aircraft. |

1962

| April 7 | Arrival in country of first two Israeli Mirage IIICJs, given the IDF/AF name Shahak (Skyblazer). |
| May | Egyptian Air Force (EAF) service introduction of MiG-21F-13. |

1964

| November 13 | Water War escalation, with IDF/AF launching massive attacks against Syria. |
| November 14 | First MiG-21F versus Mirage IIICJ aerial combat ends inconclusively. |

1965

| Spring | Algerian Air Force MiG-21F-13 service introduction. |
| Summer | EAF receives first examples of 45-50 improved MiG-21FLs. |

1966

July 14	First air-to-air kill in MiG-21 versus Mirage III engagement when No. 101 Sqn pilot Yoram Agmon destroys a SyAAF MiG-21.
August 16	IrAF MiG-21 pilot Munir Radfa defects to Israel with his aircraft, flying from Rashid to Hatzor.
November 13	IDF/AF launches Operation *Grinder* reprisal attack against Jordan.

1967

| April 7 | A major Water War clash between Israel and Syria results in Shahak pilots credited with six MiG-21 kills. SyAAF admitted loss of four MiG-21s and claimed five IDF/AF aircraft shot down. |
| May 15 | Israel stages Independence Day march in demilitarised Jerusalem. Egyptian armed forces march into UNEF-occupied Sinai. |

Symbols of early 1960s Egyptian air power fly in formation during a ceremonial flypast over Cairo in 1965. The two MiG-21F-13s are escorting a Tu-16 armed with two AS-1 "Kennel" air-to-ground missiles. By June 5, 1967, Egypt possessed 299 combat aircraft, 102 of which were MiG-21s.

June 5	IDF/AF launches pre-emptive strike on EAF bases in order to win air superiority over Sinai Desert. Shahak pilots claim six kills in first wave of attacks, and by day's end their tally has risen to 19 victories (including ten MiG-21s). First Shahak lost to enemy fighters falls to EAF MiG-21 on this day too.
June 6	Shahak units claim 13.5 victories, (three of them MiG-21s).
June 7	Shahak units claim seven victories, although none are MiG-21s.
June 8	Shahak units claim eight victories, (two of them MiG-21s).
June 9	Shahak units claim final three victories of Six Day War, with last kill being a SyAAF MiG-21.
June 10	IDF/AF admit the loss of nine Shahaks in Six Day War, four of which were downed as a result of aerial combat. Only two allegedly shot down by Arab fighters, the rest being lost to anti-aircraft artillery (AAA) fire, SA-2s, fuel starvation or combat debris.

DESIGN AND DEVELOPMENT

MIRAGE III

The driving force behind Dassault, Marcel Bloch was born in Paris on January 22, 1892. Having become aware of aviation in 1909 after he saw his first aeroplane, Bloch subsequently studied electrical engineering at the Ecole Breguet. He then enrolled in the prestigious Ecole Superieure d'Aeronautique et de Construction Mecanique (SUPAERO), which was the world's first dedicated aerospace engineering school, in 1912-13. Whilst Bloch was there, one of his classmates was Russian Mikhail Gurevich, who later teamed up with the Artyem Mikoyan in October 1939 to create the legendary design bureau MiG.

Bloch worked in the French Aeronautics Research Laboratory during World War 1 and then established the Societe des Avions Marcel Bloch, which produced its first aircraft in 1930. Having created parts for the national aircraft industry, Bloch's company was nationalised on January 16, 1937 and became part of the Societe Nationale de Constructions Aeronautiques de Sud-Ouest.

The occupation of France by the Germans in World War II had a devastating effect on the country's aviation industry in general and on Bloch in particular, for he was imprisoned from October 5, 1940 until August 17, 1944, when he was transported to Buchenwald concentration camp in Germany. Having refused to cooperate with his German captors, Bloch was due to be hung, but French Communist Party activists saved him by swapping his identity with a fellow prisoner who had died just a few hours before the execution. Buchenwald was liberated in April 1945 and Bloch set about resurrecting his aircraft business. Born a Jew, he converted to Catholicism and changed his name to Marcel Dassault (which loosely translated into the word "Tank"). Dassault had been the alias of his elder brother, French Resistance leader Gen Darius Paul Bloch, during World War II. Avions Marcel Bloch was duly renamed Avions Marcel Dassault on January 20, 1947.

Two years later Dassault's Ouragan jet fighter flew for the first time, thus establishing the company as the leading French manufacturer of jet fighters. Its stable of aircraft progressively developed from the subsonic Ouragan, via the transonic Mystere (first flown in 1951) to the supersonic Super Mystere (first flown in 1955). The Mystere-Delta also commenced flight testing in 1955.

Straight wings (as fitted to the American F-104 Starfighter), swept wings (as fitted to the British Lightning) and delta wing configurations were all explored by aerospace engineers in the 1950s as they strived to develop the next generation of Mach 2-capable jet fighters. Dassault decided that the delta wing configuration would best suit a French Mach 2 fighter, primarily because locally produced jet engines lacked the thrust generated by contemporary American and British powerplants. Development of the Dassault delta fighter commenced in 1951, with a production contract being received from the French government on February 27, 1952.

The Mystere-Delta was initially designed to weigh nine tons. However, lessons learned from early jet fighter combat in the Korean War raised concerns as to both the cost and the size of future combat aircraft, since the relatively cheap six-ton Soviet MiG-15 had proven to be more than a match for the appreciably more expensive, and heavier, eight-ton American F-86 Sabre. Therefore, in early 1953, the *Armée de l'Air* issued a revised requirement for a lightweight interceptor. Dassault put forward two four-ton designs, namely the MD 550, powered by two small turbojets and one powerful rocket motor, and the MD 560 that boasted a single powerful turbojet and a smaller booster rocket. The envisaged mission profile was a climb to 49,000ft in less than five minutes, accelerating with the rocket booster from Mach 1.1 at 32,000ft to Mach 1.4 at 49,000ft. The rocket motor would flame out at this point, leaving the pilot of the lightweight fighter to chase down his target – probably an enemy bomber flying at Mach 1 – using a single air-to-air missile (AAM).

The IDF/AF evaluated several examples of the ten Mirage IIIA pre-series fighters in France in October-November 1959 and concluded that the delta fighter was suitable for multi-role combat. However, at that time the Mirage III had only three hard-points – here, the aircraft is fitted with rocket pods under the wings. Standing in front of the jet is IDF/AF Chief Test Pilot Danny Shapira, who has just returned from a sortie. The fighter's versatility was greatly enhanced when two more hard-points were added beneath the outer wing sections.

The *Armeé de l'Air* rejected the MD 560 proposal in June 1953 and ordered two MD 550 prototypes to be constructed three months later. Development of the aircraft's locally built turbojet engine lagged behind schedule, so when the prototype Mystere-Delta first flew on June 25, 1955 it was powered by two British Armstrong Siddeley Vipers, each rated at 2,160lbs st. Initial flight-testing showed that the aircraft was promising enough to prompt a change of name – it became the Mirage I. With the fighter adorned with its new monicker on its nose, the MD 550 made the first of a series of flights with afterburning Vipers in May 1956.

Although the aircraft went supersonic in a dive during one such sortie on May 29, the Mirage I was clearly unsuited to the role of point defence interceptor because its engines lacked sufficient thrust to sustain Mach 1+ speeds in level flight for any period of time. Indeed, it only achieved its maximum speed of Mach 1.6 thanks to the installation of a SEPR 66 bi-fuel rocket motor that burnt for a mere 20 seconds. The airframe was also too small for the fighter to carry an effective military load, and the pilot had to rely on a ground network of radar stations in order to intercept an enemy target – there was no room in the MD 550 for a radar. Finally, insufficient knowledge in respect to aerodynamics and propulsion limited the aircraft's theoretical top speed to Mach 1.4, which was not fast enough to counter supersonic bombers then under development in the USSR.

Dassault had realised the limitations of the lightweight interceptor early on, and in March 1956 it proposed two heavier Mirage variants. The Mirage III was a single-engined delta-winged fighter, while the Mirage IV was a larger twin-engined version that would ultimately serve with the *Armeé de l'Air* as a nuclear bomber.

The interaction between Dassault and the *Armeé de l'Air* eventually generated a new operational requirement, issued on September 3, 1956, for an all-weather interceptor. The principal threat that the aircraft had been designed to oppose was a supersonic bomber cruising at altitudes between 39,000ft and 66,000ft. The projected all-weather interceptor was no longer a lightweight fighter as had originally been envisaged with the MD 550, as it now featured an integral weapon system (including

MIRAGE IIICJ

48ft 3.8in.

13ft 11.5in.

26ft 11.5in.

radar) and more fuel. Two light interceptor features were retained, however – a rocket booster (this time only for interception profiles against targets cruising at 66,000ft) and an armament of just a single AAM.

On November 15, 1956, the *Armeé de l'Air* informed Dassault that both of its revised Mirage proposals had been accepted, but that the Mirage IV would be modified to serve as a bomber, while the Mirage III would be developed as an all-weather interceptor. Dassault had clearly been informed of this decision well ahead of it being officially announced, for the prototype seven-ton Mirage III 001 made its first flight just 48 hours later! Powered by an interim SNECMA Atar 101G turbojet engine, the prototype's construction had been accelerated through use of components from the second prototype of the abandoned Mirage I. Flight testing also progressed rapidly, with the speed of sound broken in level flight on just its second sortie, afterburner ignition on the third and supersonic flight (Mach 1.24) registered during the fourth hop.

The new all-weather interceptor was indeed powerful enough for the projected mission profile and heavy enough to accommodate the planned weapon system. Yet testing revealed a speed barrier of Mach 1.4 that was only exceeded by the ignition of the SEPR 66 booster rocket. With the latter, speeds close to Mach 1.9 could be achieved, but the design objective figure of Mach 2 remained elusive primarily because the prototype lacked a sufficiently powerful engine and suitably advanced aerodynamics.

The Mirage III 001 was grounded for modifications on December 20, 1957. The most important of these was the fitment of moveable shock cones, known to the French as "Mice" (Souris), within the air intakes to control the airflow into the engine. The shock cones moved forward as supersonic speed increased, thus keeping the airflow subsonic at the throat of the intake. The moveable cones kept the shock waves at their optimum velocity throughout the supersonic speed range, thus allowing the engine to produce maximum power. The modified Mirage III 001 returned to the air on April 17, 1958, and 25 days later the first pre-production Mirage IIIA01 made its maiden flight. Powered by the SNECMA Atar 09B, which was rated at 13,230lbs st with afterburner, the shock cone-equipped Mirage IIIA01 became the first European aircraft to fly faster than Mach 2 in level flight on October 24, 1958. Such performance fully justified Dassault's selection of the delta wing configuration to compensate for the Mirage III's lack of thrust.

By then the new Mach 2 fighter had evolved into a family of combat aircraft. Following an initial *Armeé de l'Air* commitment for 100 Mirage IIIA point defence interceptors, the Mirage IIIB two-seat trainer was ordered on February 25, 1958. The latter had a lengthened fuselage to allow a second cockpit to be inserted in place of fuel and radio equipment, which was in turn relocated in the nose section in place of the Thomson CSF fire control radar. First flown on October 20, 1959, the Mirage IIIB was rated as combat capable despite having no radar, reduced fuel and cannon armament that could only be fitted after internal rear cockpit equipment had been removed.

With weapon system development lagging badly behind aerodynamics, airframe construction and propulsion, Dassault was informed by the *Armeé de l'Air* on

August 8, 1958 that the Mirage IIIA would not progress to full-scale production. Instead, a new interceptor variant was launched in the form of the Mirage IIIC, the first example of which made its maiden flight on October 9, 1960.

Compared with the eight-ton pre-production Mirage IIIA, the 12-ton Mirage IIIC was a production-standard combat aircraft armed with a fully functioning, if still technologically immature, weapon system. Equipped with a Cyrano radar, armed with Matra R 530 semi-active radar homing AAMs and featuring an Atar 09B engine and SEPR 84 booster rocket, the Mirage IIIC was designed to be used exclusively as an interceptor. However, the original baseline interception profile that had shaped its construction was already obsolete by the time the *Armeé de l'Air* gave the aircraft its service introduction on July 7, 1961. The deployment of effective surface-to-air missiles had forced a change in the way bombers penetrated enemy airspace. Instead of approaching at high altitude, they were now forced to attack at low altitude in order to avoid the SAM threat. The introduction of intercontinental ballistic missiles had also reduced the importance of the strategic bomber, while the creation of the mutual deterrence policy between the USSR and the USA, and its Western allies, made an atomic war a highly unlikely scenario.

No longer required to serve purely as an interceptor, the Mirage IIIC was quickly developed into a multi-role air-to-air fighter by Dassault. The SEPR 84 rocket was discarded in favour of more fuel and two DEFA 552 30mm cannon with 125 rounds per gun – the latter were housed in a ventral gun pack. However, the Mirage IIIC initially lacked a short-range infrared-homing AAM to bridge the gap between the cannon and the R 530. With hindsight, this was not a handicap as all early infrared-homing AAMs proved to be far from effective weapons.

Further variants soon followed the Mirage IIIC along the Dassault production line, with the low-level penetration attack mission being the domain of the Mirage IIIE and photo-reconnaissance performed by the Mirage IIIR. Both were ordered into production for the *Armeé de l'Air* on April 6, 1960, with the Mirage IIIE first flying on April 5, 1961 and the Mirage IIIR on October 31, 1961. The Mirage IIIE was slightly longer to provide additional fuselage volume for avionics and fuel. Powered

Although all 72 Mirage IIICJs were built exactly the same way in France, some subsequently accrued a better reputation in combat than others. Shahak (?)55 (seen here closest to the camera), for example, was believed to be a "jinxed jet" as its guns always jammed in combat, resulting in the fighter never being credited with an air-to-air kill. On October 10, 1968, the aircraft crashed on landing, severely injuring No. 119 Sqn pilot Shamuel Ben-Rom. Rebuilt, Shahak 55 suffered engine failure and again crash-landed on March 4, 1971, severely injuring No. 101 Sqn pilot Yermi Keidar. This time it was not rebuilt.

by the Atar 09C-3 (which produced the same thrust as the Atar 09B – 13,668lbs st – but incorporated design improvements, especially in the afterburner section), the Mirage IIIE was conceived as a tactical nuclear bomber, but mostly served as a conventional multi-role combat aircraft. Along with the companion Mirage IIID two-seater and simplified Mirage 5, the Mirage IIIE accounted for the bulk of the 1,422 Mirage IIIs built by Dassault or under licence in Australia and Switzerland.

France ordered a total of 419 Mirage fighters – the Mirage I and III prototypes, ten pre-production Mirage IIIAs, 59 Mirage IIIB trainers, 95 Mirage IIIC interceptors, 183 Mirage IIIE fighter-bombers and 70 Mirage IIIR photo-reconnaissance aircraft. The balance of the production run was manufactured for export, as the Dassault delta dominated foreign markets across the globe. Indeed, of all the Mach 2 fighters designed in the West during the 1950s, only the American F-4 Phantom II and F-104 Starfighter were exported in similar numbers to the Mirage III.

Ironically, exports of the French delta fighter started rather slowly, with the first attempt to export the Mirage III ending in bitter disappointment when West Germany selected the F-104 instead, ordering no fewer than 700 examples in October 1958. Israel subsequently became the first export customer for the Mirage III, and it was the IDF/AF's combat record that generated sales of the aircraft from the late 1960s. Indeed, only a third of the eventual Mirage III/5 export total had been ordered prior to the June 1967 Six Day War. The aircraft's success in this conflict generated sales to air arms in western Europe, Africa and South America as customers purchased the Mirage III/5 to perform the attack, reconnaissance and, above all else, air superiority mission following its defeat of the standard Mach 2-capable fighter threat of the era, the Soviet MiG-21.

MiG-21

The Mikoyan-Gurevich MiG-21 was the Mach 2 successor of the subsonic MiG-9, the transonic MiG-15 and MiG-17 and the supersonic MiG-19, just as the Mirage III had evolved from the subsonic Ouragan, the transonic Mystere and the supersonic Super Mystere. Of all the Mach 2 fighters developed in the early 1950s, the MiG-21 and the Mirage III had more in common than any other pair. They were created over a similar timeframe in a development process that shared many concepts – both were expected to overcome propulsion weakness through light weight and fine-tuned aerodynamics. As a result, the MiG-21 and the Mirage III had comparable performance, despite the latter boasting a delta wing while the Soviet fighter had both a delta wing and a conventional tailplane.

Artyem Mikoyan was born in 1905 in Armenia, which was then part of the Russian Empire. Once of employable age, he initially worked as a machine tool operator. In 1937 Mikoyan graduated from the Zhukovsky Air Force Academy and secured a position with the highly successful Polikarpov design bureau, where Mikhail Gurevich was employed as a senior design team leader. The latter's background was utterly

MiG-21F-13

51ft 8.5in.

13ft 5.3in.

23ft 5.5in.

different to Mikoyan's. Born in 1893, Gurevich had been expelled from Kharkov University (where he had been studying mathematics from 1910) following his participation in revolutionary activities. Travelling to France to complete his education, Gurevich graduated from SUPAERO in the same class as Marcel Dassault. He then returned to the USSR and worked in the aircraft industry as an engineer and designer until 1939, when he was assigned to share the leadership of a new design bureau named Mikoyan-Gurevich, which was abbreviated to MiG.

The state-owned Soviet aerospace industry was set up whereby research, design and mass production were all carried out separately. The Central Aerodynamics and Hydrodynamics Institute (CAHI) conveyed knowledge to the Experimental Construction (design) bureaus, who used this information to shape their aircraft designs which, if successful, were put into production at various factories spread across the USSR.

When the time was right for the development of Mach 2 fighters, the CAHI explored possible configurations and concluded that the best options for achieving such speeds would be either sharply swept-back or delta wings. Both would ensure speeds in excess of Mach 2, with sufficient strength and stiffness, reasonable manoeuvrability and acceptable take-off and landing characteristics. The Soviet aerodynamicists were against pure delta configurations, however, endorsing a smaller delta wing with conventional all-moving horizontal tailplanes.

MiG explored the practicality of CAHI's aerodynamic recommendations through the development and testing of two similar prototypes, one of which (Ye-2) had sharply swept-back wings and the other (Ye-4) delta wings and all-moving horizontal tailplanes. Prototype design started in 1954, and the Ye-2 became the first to fly on February 14, 1955. The latter machine's fuselage closely resembled that eventually adopted for the MiG-21, being both compact and simple. The fighter featured a nose-mounted air intake which, although a boon when it came to mass-production, restricted the size of the aircraft's radar. Radar range was a function of antenna dish size, so the smaller the

This Iraqi Air Force MiG-21F-13 was flown to Israel by defector Capt Munir Radfa on August 12, 1966. Quickly repainted with IDF/AF markings, the fighter was given an in-flight evaluation between September and November 1966. Data from these sorties was presented to Israeli fighter pilots, but the latter did not get the chance to fly dissimilar air combat with the jet. Such a decision was highly criticised by frontline pilots at the time, and this policy was duly changed in 1968 after the IDF/AF obtained two airworthy MiG-17s. Indeed, most, it not all, Israeli pilots flew training missions against the latter jets.

dish the more modest its performance. Such compromise was acceptable at the time, however, because fellow Soviet design bureau Sukhoi was developing the Su-9 heavy interceptor (in the same class as the American F-106) with a larger radar. The MiG-21 did not suffer too much from the performance of its radar because Ground Control Intercept (GCI) would, in the main, support combat operations.

The Ye-4 development airframe made its first flight on June 16, 1955, this aircraft being in many ways the Soviet equivalent of the French Mirage I. Both prototypes had flown within ten days of each other, both boasted engines rated at 7,165lbs st thrust, both were limited to Mach 1.4 and both subsequently proved their respective aerodynamic configurations to the point of selection for mass production.

Although both types had flown in June 1955, the Soviet project soon forged ahead. On January 9, 1956, the moveable shock cone-equipped Ye-5 made its first flight, powered by a Tumanski AM-11 (R-11) turbojet engine rated at 11,243lbs st. This event took place almost a year ahead of the equivalent Mirage III 001. While both Dassault and MiG emphasised small size, light weight and aerodynamic efficiency to offset a lack of propulsion, the French opted for elegant solutions while the Soviets embraced simplicity. For example, when devising a solution to in-flight instability problems caused by local airflow separation over the wings, the MiG team simply fitted wing fences. Dassault, however, opted for notches to preserve the elegant look of the smooth delta wing.

The timelines for MiG-21 and Mirage III development again converged in May 1958 when the first pre-production examples of both types (known, respectively, as the Ye-6 and Mirage IIIA) took to the air for the first time. Unlike the Mach 2 Mirage IIIA, the Ye-6 could only manage Mach 1.95 in level flight. Once in service, achieving Mach 2 horizontally in either the MiG-21 or the Mirage III was a tough task due to the added weight and drag of external stores such as missiles and drop tanks. This had little effect on the aircrafts' "combatability", however, as they mostly flew, and fought, in the Mach 0.5-1.5 speed range.

The pre-production Ye-6 quickly evolved into the production standard MiG-21F, which was fitted with an SRD-5M Kvant (Quantum) radar, had a broader vertical tail and was powered by an R-11F-300 fully variable afterburning engine that generated 12,655lbs st thrust. Mass production commenced at Gorky in late 1959 and Soviet air force service introduction followed in March 1960. The MiG-21F was a daytime tactical multi-role combat aircraft rather than an all-weather interceptor like the Mirage IIIC or an interdictor like the Mirage IIIE.

Armed with two internal Nudelman-Richter NR-30 30mm cannon, with 60 rounds per gun, and equipped with three hard-points, the MiG-21F's external load was limited to a fuel tank under the fuselage and two weapons (bombs or rockets) under the wings. AAM armament was introduced in 1960 in the form of the infrared-homing R-3S, which was a Soviet copy of the American AIM-9B Sidewinder. To compensate for the added weight of the

A "finger-four" of MiG-21F-13s from the EAF in 1964, these aircraft probably hailing from the first Egyptian unit to be issued with the "Fishbed-C".

AAMs, only a single cannon and magazine of just 30 rounds were retained. NATO reporting names for the new fighter and its AAM were "Fishbed-C" and AA-2 "Atoll".

As previously noted, the modest internal volume of the MiG-21F's nose cone precluded the insertion of a more capable radar system. The aircraft was duly equipped with the SRD-5M Kvant range radar that was adequate for the tactical role fulfilled by this basic day fighter. An all-weather interceptor variant of the MiG-21 that was developed as a light-weight complement to the larger Sukhoi family of interceptors first flew as the Ye-7 on August 10, 1958. Given the service designation MiG-21P, the interceptor had a dorsal spine and a re-shaped nose section that featured an enlarged fixed conical centrebody housing a more advanced TsD-30T fire control radar. As with virtually all interceptors at this time, the MiG-21P was armed exclusively with AAMs – the solitary cannon had been removed to offset the added weight of the more advanced avionics. Put into production in mid-1960, the MiG-21P was replaced by the re-engined MiG-21PF two years later.

A plethora of fighter models followed throughout the 1960s, complemented in 1966 by the MiG-21R reconnaissance aircraft and more advanced versions of the MiG-21U two-seat trainer – the first of these had flown on October 17, 1960. Numerous MiG-21 versions developed henceforth fall outside the coverage of this volume, which deals with variants in service in the Middle East up to mid-1967.

All in all, three Soviet fighter factories manufactured more than 12,300 MiG-21s, while license production accounted for an additional 194 aircraft in Czechoslovakia and 657 in India. Overall, more than 13,000 airframes had been built by the time Soviet production ended in 1986. MiG-21 variants remained in production in China for many years after that, however.

From a numerical perspective, the MiG-21 was significantly more prolific than the Mirage III. Both fighters enjoyed considerable success in the export market, with 70 percent of the Mirage IIIs built being sold to foreign customers. For the MiG-21, the figure was probably closer to 30 percent, which in turn meant that about 1,000 Mirage IIIs and some 4,000 MiG-21s were exported worldwide. Many of these aircraft found their way to the Middle East, where the two types initially clashed in 1964 and eventually fought a full-scale war in June 1967.

Following its evaluation by the IDF/AF, the ex-IrAF MiG-21F-13 was painted in high-visibility colours, armed with two early pre-production Shafrir 2 AAMs and assigned the quick reaction alert mission. It is seen here on duty outside No 101 Sqn's QRA complex at Hatzor in mid-1967, ready to intercept high-flying Egyptian MiG-21s that were virtually immune to interception by Israeli Mirage IIICJs.

TECHNICAL
SPECIFICATIONS

IDF/AF MIRAGE IIICJ 1962–67

Procurement of the Mirage IIIC was the logical next step for the IDF/AF following its acquisition of the Ouragan in 1955, the Mystere in 1956 and the Super Mystere in 1958. Israel initially began exploring the Mirage III option in February 1957 when the delta-winged fighter project was presented to Ministry of Defence Chief Executive Officer Shimon Peres during a visit to France. The IDF General Staff discussed the Mirage III for future service on May 11, 1957, and on November 30, 1958 Chief of Staff Haim Laskov ordered the fighter to be evaluated. The Mirage III had been presented to the Israelis as a point defence interceptor optimised for high altitude operations. As such, IDF chiefs were of the view that it added little to the air force's tactical operations, which at that time were mostly flown at low to medium altitudes. Laskov therefore recommended that only a single squadron of Mirage IIIs be acquired.

A massive IDF/AF staff study into the merits of the aircraft commenced, this being divided into a technical evaluation and order of battle plan that were aimed at challenging Laskov's dictum that only a single squadron's worth of fighters should be bought because the Mirage III was not a multi-role combat aircraft. The technical evaluation covered operational requirements and the theoretical assessment of a Mach 2 multi-role combat aircraft equipped with an advanced navigation system and designed for Short Take-Off and Landing (STOL). Obviously, the Mirage III variant of 1957 was not multi-role, lacked an advanced navigation system and had no STOL capability!

The IDF/AF assessment of the Mirage III was forwarded to the IDF Chief of Staff on March 4, 1959, the Dassault machine being presented as a multi-role combat

IDF/AF Chief Test Pilot Danny Shapira poses with the Mirage IIIA03 during familiarisation flights in June 1959. Shapira had earned his IDF/AF wings in 1949 and had graduated from the *Armeé de l'Air's* test pilots' school in 1959.

aircraft. Only two changes were specified to give the aircraft a multi-role capability, and thus make it more appealing to Laskov and his staff. The Mirage III needed to have five rather then three external hard points and a magazine that housed 250 rounds of 30mm ammunition per gun – a figure that IDF/AF experts viewed as inadequate for the multi-role mission. Dassault did eventually add two more hardpoints, but the ammunition for the DEFA 552 cannon remained at just 125 rounds per gun.

Once the multi-role potential of the Mirage III had been established, it was possible to challenge the IDF chief of staff's one squadron dictum. However, theoretical reports did not impress Laskov, so the next step in the IDF/AF's Mirage III acquisition process was the flight evaluation performed by its Chief Test Pilot Danny Shapira. He flew the aircraft for the first time on June 23, 1959, and his third and final flight in this test phase also included a Mach 2 dash on June 26. A more extensive evaluation followed in October-November 1959, when Shapira made 18 flights that included weapons testing (six sorties) and rocket zoom-climbs (two sorties). His report lavished praise on the Mirage III, and he noted that the aircraft was "well suited for modification into a multi-role platform that would make it clearly superior to all other IDF/AF combat aircraft types".

Shapira's evaluation convinced Laskov that the Mirage III was indeed more than a high-altitude interceptor, and therefore eligible for acquisition in significant numbers. He duly notified Prime Minister David Ben-Gurion on November 10, 1959 of an operational requirement for 60 Mirage IIIs. The Israeli government in turn forwarded to France a request for the acquisition of 60 Dassault fighters – 30 confirmed and 30 as an option, based on the original French credit agreement of payment over just four years. During subsequent negotiations Dassault offered Israel less generous credit terms so that the May 1960 contract signed between the two parties covered the supply of 60 Mirage IIIs, only 24 of which were confirmed. The option deadline for the remaining 36 aircraft was March 31, 1961, and deliveries were scheduled to start six months later. Israel exercised the option, but the April 28, 1961 contract covered only an additional 24 aircraft because of limited funds. The option on the remaining 12 aircraft was extended to September 15, 1961, by which point the IDF/AF had stated that it actually had an operational requirement for 90 Mirage IIIs to equip three 24-aircraft squadrons, and still have adequate reserves for attrition and maintenance.

ה „יהלום"   ה „שפריר"

IDF/AF Commander Maj Gen Ezer Weizman assigned top priority to frontline squadrons having adequate numbers of aircraft, and he suggested cancellation of the Mirage IIICJ's SEPR rocket and Matra R 530 semi-active radar homing AAM so as to fund the acquisition of an additional 42 jets. This proposition was never accepted, but a third 24-aircraft increment was approved by the time the September 15, 1961 option lapsed, thus bringing the total Israeli Mirage IIICJ buy to 72 airframes.

The first two aircraft landed at Hatzor air base on April 7, 1962 and were issued to No. 101 Sqn, at which point the fighter was given the Hebrew name Shahak (Skyblazer). Deliveries to Ramat David-based No. 117 Sqn commenced on July 7, 1962, while the third Shahak unit, No. 119 Sqn at Tel Nof, received its final examples on July 28, 1964. That same year Israel ordered three Mirage IIIBJ combat-capable trainers, the two-seaters being delivered to Israel in February, March and April 1966 – a single example was issued to each of the Shahak squadrons. By April 1, 1967, the Shahak force accounted for 33 percent of the IDF/AF's total fighter strength.

As Maj Gen Weizman had recommended, SEPR rocket acquisition was indeed rejected, but the IDF/AF went ahead with the limited purchase of the R 530 semi-active radar homing AAM to augment the indigenous Rafael Shafrir (Dragonfly) infrared-homing AAM. Israeli acquisition of the R 530, christened Yahalom (Diamond), covered the purchase of 15 missiles, three training rounds and eight launch pylons. Missiles were issued to Nos. 101 and 117 Sqns for their Quick Reaction Alert (QRA) aircraft. Both squadrons achieved Yahalom qualification in 1964, the weapon's engagement envelope being 360 degrees against a target flying

The Shahak's QRA air-to-air mission configuration included a single Matra R 530 Yahalom semi-active radar-homing AAM under the fuselage and a Rafael Shafrir infrared-homing AAM on each of the outer wing pylons. As this photograph clearly shows, No. 101 Sqn Shahaks had their rudders marked up with red and white stripes from July 1963.

The Shafrir 2 was developed by Rafael to replace the less than successful Shafrir 1 as the IDF/AF's principal infrared AAM. Appreciably larger than the company's original short-range missile, the Shafrir 2 achieved service introduction in 1969. This particular weapon, however, was one of a series of development rounds built for testing and launched from the ex-IrAF MiG-21F-13 during trials in 1967.

higher than 30,000ft over land or 10,000ft over sea, and a rear hemisphere launch only against a target flying at a lower altitude. R 530 engagement range was one to ten miles, but radar lock had to be achieved prior to launch, and this proved difficult in a combat situation with the unsophisticated Cyrano system fitted in the Mirage IIICJ.

Supplementing the Yahalom in close combat was the Shafrir, which could be fired at distances of up to two miles at high altitude, one mile at medium altitude and a

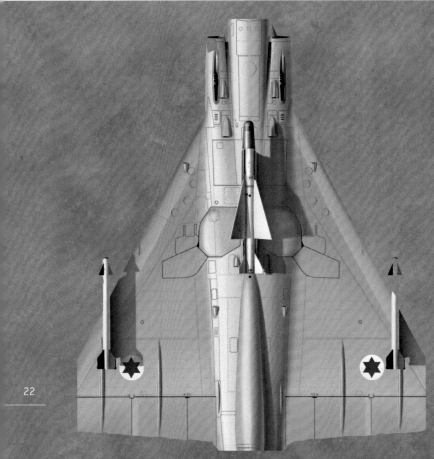

MIRAGE IIICJ MISSILES

During the Six Day War, the Shahak's external air-to-air weapon options consisted of either the locally developed Rafael Shafrir 1 infrared AAM and/or the French-built Matra R 530 semi-active radar-homing AAM. The former, weighing just 37kg and armed with a 3.5kg warhead, was always carried on the outer wing stations. The R 530, weighing 195kg and armed with a 27kg warhead, was mounted on the centreline station. Both weapons proved to be a huge disappointment in combat.

Shahak 52's victory tally is clearly visible in this close-up in flight view taken sometime after the April 7, 1967 action involving SyAAF MiG-21s. Iftach Spector shared his second claim in the jet with Beni Romach, flying Shahak 57. The Mirage IIICJ's cannon troughs are also well illustrated from this angle.

minimum distance of 500 metres at low altitude. This weapon was issued to Nos. 101 and 117 Sqns for their night QRA aircraft from May 1963 and day QRA three months later, while No. 119 Sqn became Shafrir qualified from February 1, 1965. The rear hemisphere Shafrir was initially considered to be the ultimate Shahak air-to-air weapon, as it was better suited to dogfighting than the Yahalom and, in theory at least, superior to the fighter's twin 30mm cannon armament. Success with the latter

MIRAGE IIICJ CANNON PACK

The Shahak's internal armament consisted of a DEFA 552 30mm cannon pack with 125 rounds per gun. Each weapon weighed 80kg and fired 20 0.27kg rounds per second at a muzzle velocity of 800 metres per second. The only drawback with this weapon was that spent cannon rounds and their associated hot exhaust gases were purged from the jet immediately below the engine air intakes. The gases could be ingested down the intakes, thus depriving the engine of oxygen and causing a compressor stall or flameout. The solution to this problem was an engine control logic that slashed the fuel feed to the powerplant when the cannon fired, thus preserving an acceptable fuel-to-oxygen mix and preventing a flameout.

Three No. 101 Sqn MiG-killers sit side-by-side in the Hatzor QRA complex on April 13, 1967. All of them have been prepared to fly the QRA mission, but they each have a different missile configuration. To left, Shahak 52 has a single Yahalom, in the centre Shahak 57 has a Shafrir under each wing, and to the right, Shahak (2)59 boasts a solitary Shafrir beneath its right wing. Iftach Spector and Beni Romach were at the controls of Shahaks 52 and 57, respectively, on April 7, 1967 when they shared in the destruction of two SyAAF MiG-21s, while Yoram Agmon used Shahak (2)59 to claim the Mirage IIICJ's first "Fishbed" kill on July 14, 1966.

weapon was dependent on radar lock and precise aiming, whereas the Shafrir could be launched from a higher nose-off angle (of up to 30 degrees) to the target and when the Mirage IIICJ was flying at faster speeds.

In order to achieve the best results with the Yahalom and Shafrir, Shahak pilots depended on GCI to manoeuvre them into a "first shot" position. The major drawback of the new AAM era was that the Shahaks were armed with only two to three missiles. Cannon was therefore still treated as a viable back-up weapon to complement the AAMs in close range engagements. The twin DEFA 552 weapons were effective from distances of 700 metres down to 100 metres, although pilots rarely dared to open fire at less than 200 metres for fear of suffering damage from debris shot off their target. The 250 rounds carried by the Shahak could generate some seven seconds worth of fire, augmenting the jet's two to three missiles.

Theoretically at least, the Shahak was well equipped for combat at distances from ten miles down to 100 metres. In reality, however, this proved not to be the case because of the gap between planned and actual weapon system performance due to the immature nature of the fighter's radar and AAM technology. Suffering from poor serviceability, both the Yahalom and Shafrir also proved unable to cope with

The Mirage IIICJ's only truly effective weapons during the Six Day War were its twin DEFA 552 30mm cannon, neatly housed in a ventral pack that could be lowered out of the jet for servicing and rearming.

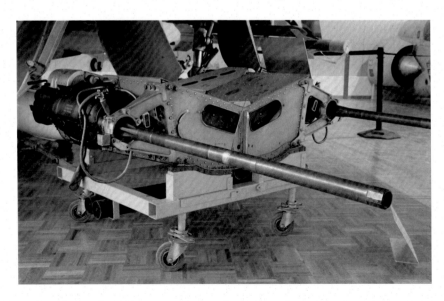

manoeuvring targets even when fully functional. Yahalom and cannon engagements were dependent upon radar lock, but the Cyrano struggled to deliver the performance promised by its manufacturer in actual combat. Indeed, ground clutter rendered both the radar and the Shafrir practically useless in low-altitude engagements.

In the early stages of its frontline career in Israel the Shahak also suffered from poor cannon accuracy due to target zeroing issues with the fighter's CSF gunsight. Initially, target hit rates during practice air-to-air gunnery drills were embarrassingly low – an average of only 1.9 percent of the rounds fired were hitting the towed target banner! Inevitably, this result was attributed to the inexperience of pilots on a new type, to the higher closing rates resulting from the Shahak's superior performance and to the deficiencies of the weapon system that made lock-on almost impossible, especially in a dogfight. The strike rate improved as pilots gained more experience with the aircraft, but the hit rate never exceeded 22 percent.

Most of these problems were caused by poor weapon system harmonisation. The CSF gunsight was slaved to the Cyrano radar, which in turn meant that the cannon could only be activated once a firing solution had been achieved by the radar when the jet was within range of the target. Since the Cyrano was unable to accurately detect range at low altitude due to ground clutter, the semi-automatic weapon system concept championed by Dassault was useless much of the time.

Manual override was therefore introduced by the IDF/AF, Shahak pilots having to estimate the range of their targets (short 250 metres, medium 400 metres and long 600 metres) prior to firing their cannon. The "Shahak Zeroing Team" devised a modification for the fighter that saw two switches installed on the control column. One provided a 250-metre range gunsight firing solution, the other fixed the sight at 400 metres, while the activation of both set it at 600 metres. In the heat of air combat pilots had only to roughly estimate the range to the target – close, medium or long – activate the appropriate switch and open fire. This step backwards in technology produced a major leap forwards in combat capabilities, although this could only be fully appreciated after the shortcomings of the promising AAM armament had been exposed in actual combat.

ARAB MiG-21F/FL "FISHBED" 1961–67

Both the Arab and Israeli purchase of Mach 2 fighters shared one common feature – the acquired type was not selected following an exhaustive competitive or evaluative process. The MiG-21 and Mirage IIIC were simply offered by the USSR and France, respectively, on a "take it or leave it" basis, as no other Mach 2-capable combat aircraft were then available to the Arab nations or Israel.

Initially at least, the Egyptian acquisition of the MiG-21F ran in parallel to the Israeli procurement of the Mirage IIICJ. As IDF/AF pilots were converting onto their new fighter in France in 1961, so their EAF counterparts were undertaking a MiG-21 conversion course in Soviet-controlled Kazakhstan. Deliveries of Shahaks to

Israel commenced in April 1962, with the first of 50 MiG-21F-13s reaching Egypt the following month. There were differences, however. While the IDF/AF equipped its fighter squadrons with 24 aircraft, the standard EAF unit was issued with just 15 jets. Like the Israelis, the Egyptians equipped three squadrons with the new fighter, two of them being based at Inshas, in the Nile Delta, and one at Cairo West – all three were reportedly subordinated to a single air brigade.

The EAF and IDF/AF also differed in respect to their organisation, as the Israelis did not divide their airspace up into zones of responsibility or have units that were the equivalent of Egyptian air brigades. The IDF/AF had only squadrons and air bases. The latter were administrative units in their own right in charge of the day-to-day running of the squadrons assigned to them, as well as base defence and logistics. However, the squadrons received their operational orders from IDF/AF headquarters, as it directly controlled all missions. The EAF's organisational structure was more complex. Although its bases functioned in a similar way administratively to their IDF/AF counterparts, the overall chain of command also included air zones and air brigades. EAF headquarters issued orders to air zones, which in turn passed them on to air brigades. To further complicate things, a MiG-21 squadron flying from one base could be subordinated to an air brigade with headquarters at another air base.

Egyptian MiG-21F-13 acquisition continued into 1964, and in January of that year IDF/AF Intelligence stated that the EAF's order of battle included 60 "Fishbed-Cs". Elsewhere in the Middle East, both Iraq and Syria had received

MiG-21F-13 CANNON

The MiG-21F-13's sole internal weapon was a single Nudelman-Richter NR-30 30mm cannon. The aircraft had gone from two NR-30 cannon to just one when it was modified to carry the R-3S "Atoll" AAM, the port weapon being replaced in its ventral housing by electronics associated with the missile. The surviving NR-30 had a magazine that housed a mere 30 rounds. The cannon weighted 65kg and fired 15 0.4kg rounds per second at a muzzle velocity of 800 metres per second. In a one second burst the NR-30 could fire 15 rounds weighing six kilograms in total, compared to the Mirage IIICJ's 40 rounds weighing 11 kilograms. The latter fighter, therefore, packed a far more powerful punch. The position of the NR-30's muzzle well aft of the nose air intake reduced the risk of engine flameout during cannon firing. The MiG-21 had an edge over the Mirage IIICJ in this respect.

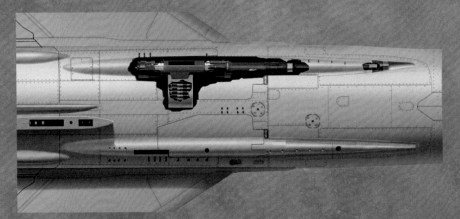

MiG-21F-13s by 1964. The IrAF would eventually take delivery of 60 "Fishbed-Cs". Finally, the Algerians also started to receive a small number of MiG-21F-13s from 1965. An updated IDF/AF Intelligence evaluation from April of that year reported Egyptian MiG-21 strength at 60 aircraft, with 30 more in Syria and 16 in Iraq. The numerical balance of power in April 1965 was, therefore, with the Arab nations, who could field 106 MiG-21s versus 67 Shahaks. The EAF activated No 40 Sqn in March 1965 at Abu Sueir, this unit becoming Egypt's fourth MiG-21 squadron.

Arab pilots praised their MiG-21F-13s for sheer performance and robust reliability. They were critical of its limited range and austere weapon system, however – both faults that also afflicted the Shahak. The MiG-21F-13's firepower consisted of just two infrared-homing R-3S "Atoll" AAMs and a single 30mm cannon that only had enough ammunition to be fired for about two seconds. The combination of these weapons gave the "Fishbed-C" a theoretical engagement range of two miles down to 100 metres.

The two Mach 2 fighters shared comparable performance, and except for the MiG-21's all-moving horizontal tailplanes, they both had a similar delta wing configuration. The horizontal tailplanes increased the wing loading for the Soviet fighter, however, despite it being lighter than the Mirage III. This in turn meant that the French aircraft enjoyed superior sustained performance in a dogfight, most prominently in horizontal manoeuvring. Thanks to its light weight, the MiG-21 had a better thrust-to-weight ratio, giving it an advantage in vertical manoeuvring.

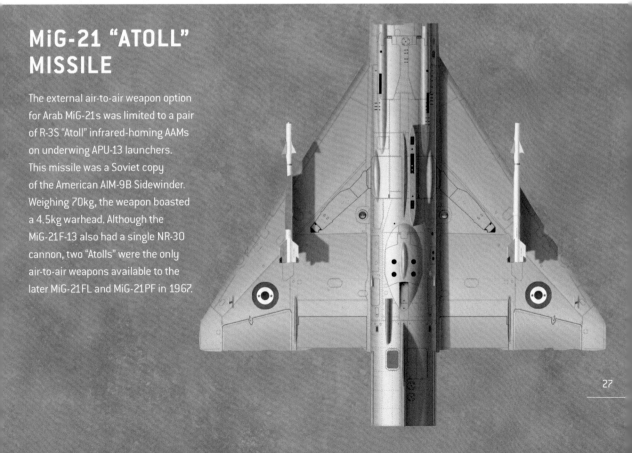

MiG-21 "ATOLL" MISSILE

The external air-to-air weapon option for Arab MiG-21s was limited to a pair of R-3S "Atoll" infrared-homing AAMs on underwing APU-13 launchers. This missile was a Soviet copy of the American AIM-9B Sidewinder. Weighing 70kg, the weapon boasted a 4.5kg warhead. Although the MiG-21F-13 also had a single NR-30 cannon, two "Atolls" were the only air-to-air weapons available to the later MiG-21FL and MiG-21PF in 1967.

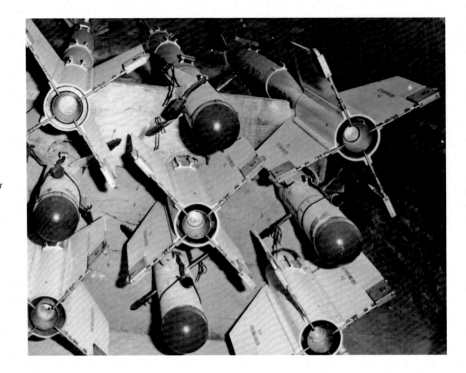

These EAF R-3S "Atoll" AAMs were captured by IDF troops at El Maliz (Bir Gafgafa) during the Six Day War. The principal weapon of Arab MiG-21s throughout the 1960s, the "Atoll" was considered to be superior to the Shafrir 1. Indeed, the Shahak was hastily modified so that it could carry these weapons in combat after their capture.

In respect to the fighters' internal fuel capacity, the MiG-21F-13 and Mirage IIICJ were closely matched at 2,480 litres and 2,550 litres, respectively. The Shahak had greater combat persistence though thanks to its three-missile/twin-gun armament, the latter capable of firing twice as many rounds from the larger magazine fitted in the fighter's gun pack. The Shahak's superiority in this area increased still further with the introduction of the MiG-21FL in the Middle East. The latter was slightly heavier than the MiG-21F-13 thanks to its improved avionics (primarily an RP-21 Spfir (Sapphire) AI radar), so the Soviet fighter's marginal thrust-to-weight ratio advantage over the Shahak disappeared.

Egypt received the first of its 45 to 50 MiG-21FLs in 1965, and these reached operational status the following year. The designation FL was used both by an export version of the MiG-21PFM and a variant manufactured in India. However, the PFM and the Indian-built FL had a twin-barrelled Gsh-23 23mm cannon in an externally mounted pod beneath the fuselage. The MiG-21FLs in Egypt were not fitted with these pods until after the Six Day War, being solely armed with a pair of heat-seeking R-3S missiles. They could more properly be designated MiG-21PFs. In most respects the PF was even less suited to the kind of fighting involving Arab pilots than the MiG-21F-13, which at least had reasonably good cockpit visibility and a powerful 30mm cannon. In fact they came to be seen as a disaster for the Arab air arms that flew them in 1967.

Although Arab air forces could only estimate the relative strengths and weaknesses of the MiG-21 in combat with the Mirage IIICJ prior to the clashes of 1967, the IDF/AF went into the Six Day War fully aware of just how effective a fighter the "Fishbed-C" was. On August 16, 1966, an IrAF MiG-21F-13 landed at Hatzor, thus ending a clandestine operation that had started in April 1965 when IDF/AF Commander Ezer Weizman mentioned how valuable an example of the Soviet fighter would be during a routine discussion with the Director of the Institute for Intelligence and Special Operations, better known as Mossad. Agents were ordered to track down an Arab fighter pilot willing to defect to Israel.

A candidate in the IrAF surfaced in late 1965 in the form of Capt Munir Radfa, although at that time he was operations officer of a MiG-17 squadron! By August 1966 he was flying the MiG-21 from Rashid, on the outskirts of Baghdad, so the defection operation was activated. Radfa embarked upon his epic 65-minute direct flight from Rashid to Hatzor on August 16, a pair of No. 119 Sqn Shahaks scrambling from Tel Nof to escort the MiG-21 pilot along the final leg of his flight.

The IDF/AF evaluation of the ex-Iraqi MiG-21F-13 commenced with a technical inspection of the airframe and the replacement of the original radio transceiver with a standard Israeli set. The MiG-21 received high praise for its simple, robust construction, although some of the techniques used in its building came in for criticism. Poor access to components that routinely needed changing due to their short operational life was also flagged up. For example, the IDF/AF's flight operations with the MiG-21 were routinely interrupted by the short life cycle of the fighter's tyres. With no supply of replacement parts to fall back on, the original worn-out tyres had to be regularly renewed through vulcanisation. Another MiG-21 design feature that IDF/AF experts considered to be a major weakness was the proximity of the aircraft's high-octane fuel tank for its internal starter to the environmental control system's oxygen bottle. Obviously it was impossible to aim for this small area in combat, but engineers believed that any battle damage sustained in this section of the fuselage would almost certainly cause the MiG-21 to explode.

This damaged EAF MiG-21FL was photographed at either Cairo West or Abu Sueir by a Shahak on a reconnaissance mission soon after the first wave of Israeli air strikes on the morning of June 5, 1967. With visible damage to the leading edge of its fin, the jet was in the process of being armed with UB-16 57mm rocket pods when it was strafed.

The in-flight evaluation of the IrAF aircraft started on September 13, 1966 when Chief Test Pilot Danny Shapira performed a familiarisation sortie. During a dozen flights from September 22 to November 7, 1966, the MiG-21's performance was compared to those of a Shahak flown by IDF/AF Weapons Systems Section test pilot Ezra Aharon. As expected, the MiG-21 had the upper hand when fighting vertically, while the Shahak proved superior in sustained manoeuvrability, especially at low altitudes. It was also discovered that a MiG-21 pilot had to endure a cramped cockpit with inferior visibility, and that the fighter's handling deteriorated considerably at speeds in excess of 575mph.

While the IDF/AF was busy comparing the MiG-21 to the Mirage IIICJ, Arab air forces were in the throes of building up their numerical superiority. By March 1967 an IDF/AF Intelligence evaluation stated that the EAF had six MiG-21 squadrons as follows – two at Inshas (including one equipped with the MiG-21FL) and one at Mansura, Cairo West, Fayid and Abu Sueir (the latter was also flying MiG-21FLs). The squadrons at Abu Sueir and Fayid were subordinated to Eastern Air Command, as was a rotational flight-sized MiG-21-equipped QRA detachment at El Maliz, in Sinai.

IDF/AF Intelligence figures for Arab air power on the morning of June 5, 1967 included 102 EAF MiG-21s, 60 SyAAF MiG-21s and 32 IrAF MiG-21s. The Egyptian MiG-21 force was organised into three air brigades (5 Air Brigade, which included No 40 Sqn, 7 Air Brigade and 9 Air Brigade, with the latter controlling El Maliz-deployed No 45 Sqn) located at six bases. The latter were Inshas (32 MiG-21s), Abu Sueir (19 MiG-21s), Cairo West (15 MiG-21s), Fayid (14 MiG-21s), El Maliz (14 MiG-21s) and Ghardaka (eight MiG-21s). SyAAF MiG-21s were based at Dmer (40 aircraft), Saikal (15 aircraft) and T-4 (five aircraft), while all 32 IrAF MiG-21s were at Rashid. Unknown to the Israelis at the time, the IrAF had orders to forward deploy its MiG-21s to Mafraq, in Jordan, if tensions in the Middle East escalated into war.

The ex-IrAF MiG-21 dominates a display of "war booty" inspected by Israeli Minister of Defence Moshe Dayan during his visit to Hatzor in July 1967. Still marked up in its pre-war high visibility QRA scheme, the aircraft is surrounded by captured equipment and weapons – the latter include 250kg and 500kg bombs, 57mm rockets and AA-2 "Atoll" missiles. Parked behind the aircraft is a mobile SA-2 SAM launcher – soon to be the scourge of the IDF/AF.

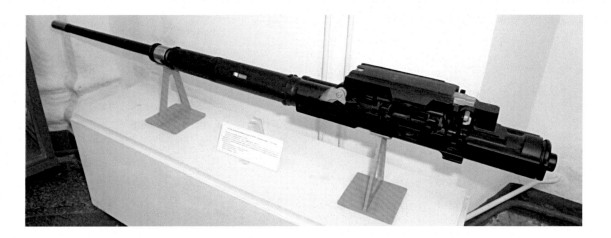

Full-scale conflict did of course commence in June 1967, by which point Israeli Shahak and Arab MiG-21 units were manned by pilots that were highly skilled, well trained and ready to wage war. Although the Arab countries initially enjoyed numerical superiority, fielding 194 MiG-21s (according to an IDF/AF Intelligence evaluation) against an Israeli force of 65 Shahaks, the latter shortened the odds considerably by only clashing with EAF aircraft during the first six hours of the Six Day War.

The MiG-21F-13's solitary internal weapon was a Nudelman-Richter NR-30 30mm cannon. It weighed 65kg and fired 15 0.4kg rounds per second at a muzzle velocity of 800 metres per second.

MiG-21F/FL AND MIRAGE IIICJ COMPARISON SPECIFICATIONS

	MiG-21F-13	MiG-21FL	Mirage IIICJ
Powerplant	1 Tumanski R-11F-300 rated at 12,654lbs st	1 Tumanski R-11F2-300 rated at 13,490lbs st	1 Atar 09B rated at 13,230lbs st
Dimensions			
Span	23ft 5.5in.	23ft 5.5in.	26ft 11.5in.
Length	51ft 8.5in. (including nose probe)	48ft 2.75in. (including nose probe)	48ft 3.8in. (including nose probe)
Height	13ft 5.3in.	13ft 5.3in.	13ft 11.5in.
Wing area	247.58 sq. ft	248.01 sq. ft	375.13 sq. ft
Weight			
Empty	10,979lb	11,587lb	13,055lb
Loaded (air combat)	19,014lb	19,334lb	21,444lb
Performance			
Max speed	1,350mph at 42,650ft	1,351mph at 41,010ft	1,386mph at 36,090ft
Range	808 miles clean	963 miles clean	745 miles clean
Climb	23,622ft per minute	23,600ft per minute	16,400ft per minute
Armament	1 x NR-30 cannon 2 x R-3S missiles	2 x R-3S missiles	2 x 30mm DEFA 552 cannon 2 x Shafrir missiles 1 x Yahalom missile

THE STRATEGIC
SITUATION

The United Arab Republic was dissolved on September 28, 1961. With Egypt heavily involved in the conflict in Yemen at the time, Syria alone faced Israel in the emerging Water War – the conflict over who controlled water resources in northern Israel, which was a major issue in the predominantly arid Middle East. Israel launched a national scheme to pipe water from the Sea of Galilee to the Negev Desert in 1953, and this project, dubbed the Israeli National Pipeline, was inaugurated on June 10, 1964. As work progressed on this scheme, tension between Israel and Syria duly increased.

In January 1964, during a diplomatic summit in Cairo, the Arab world gave its official response to the National Pipeline when it called for the launch of an Arab engineering enterprise to divert water from sources feeding the Sea of Galilee, for the establishment of a unified Arab military command and for support of the Palestine Liberation Organisation (PLO). The Water War escalated still further following the activation of the National Pipeline, and this in turn meant that the IDF/AF played an increasingly important role from November 1964. The Syrian water diversion project was vulnerable to Israeli air strikes, and this led to it being repeatedly attacked in 1965–66. The IDF/AF destroyed Syrian fortifications, artillery batteries and heavy engineering equipment with these strikes.

Syria's sponsorship of PLO attacks on Israel during this period also brought the IDF/AF into play as terrorist targets were hit too. With its ability to strike at Israel hampered by these attacks, the PLO opened a new front on November 11–12, 1966 when Jordan-based terrorists planted a mine on a road used by IDF patrols. An Israeli vehicle was destroyed and several soldiers killed in the resulting explosion. Ignoring

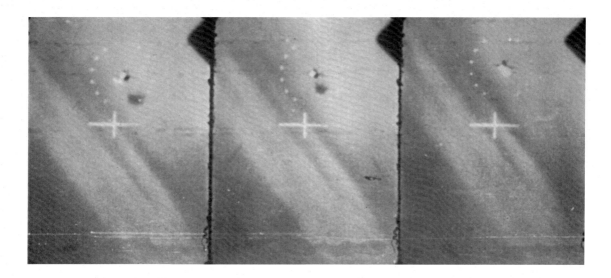

US support for the Jordan government and Soviet backing of the regime in Syria, the IDF decided to launch a major reprisal operation against PLO targets in Jordan.

Operation *Grinder* duly commenced on November 13, 1966, with strikes taking place in Jordan – a Royal Jordanian Air Force Hunter fell to a No. 119 Sqn Shahak on this date. The latter country had signed a mutual defence agreement with Egypt just nine days earlier, yet it provided very little in the way of defensive support for Jordan during *Grinder*. Indeed, the Egyptians were accused of hiding behind a screen of UNEF troops and doing nothing in the name of "Arab solidarity". An aerial clash over the Egyptian-Israeli border on November 29, 1966 damaged the EAF's shaky image still further when two MiG-19s were destroyed by Shahaks of No. 101 Sqn.

The next series of aerial engagements involving IDF/AF Mirage IIICJs and Arab MiG-21s came on April 7, 1967 over the Israeli-Syrian border when the two nations fought what could only be described as a day of "mini war". The IDF/AF flew no fewer than 171 fighter sorties and expended 65 tons of bombs. The highpoint of this

ABOVE
These gunsight camera frames from No. 101 Sqn Shahak call-sign "Heavy 1", flown by future ace Amos Amir, were taken during his November 14, 1964 engagement with a Syrian MiG-21. The black triangle indicator on the top right corner of each frame signalled that these particular images were exposed while the fighter's trigger was depressed. Cannon shells can been seen exploding in the right and left frames as both the MiG-21 and Mirage IIICJ fly a gentle left-hand turn.

LEFT
A military delegation from the EAF is introduced to the CO of an IrAF MiG-21F-13 squadron – probably the 17th – in early 1967. The delegation's visit to Iraq was part of an effort by the Arab countries in the Middle East to coordinate their air strength more effectively.

Most engagements between the MiG-21 and Mirage IIICJ prior to the Six Day War took place over the Israeli-Syrian border. During the June 1967 conflict, the EAF's five MiG-21 bases were at the top of the IDF/AF's target list, and they were all repeatedly bombed on the first morning of the war. El Maliz eventually fell into Israeli hands. Syrian bases were also targeted, as was H-3 in western Iraq. The latter site was only used as a refuelling stop for its MiG-21s, which were based at Rashid, in eastern Iraq – beyond the range of IDF/AF fighter-bombers.

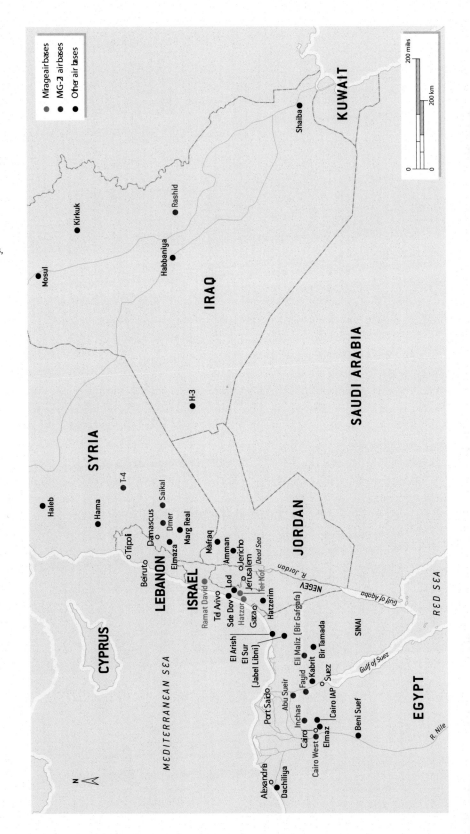

action was a series of air combats between the ultimate symbols of Arab and Israeli air power – the MiG-21F/FL and Mirage IIICJ. The IDF/AF claimed six kills, while the SyAAF admitted the loss of four MiG-21s.

The destruction of these aircraft was a serious blow to the Arab world's Soviet backers, and the dropping of so many bombs on Syria provided its allies with a stern test of their stated solidarity. Following recent humiliations in low-level clashes with Israel, the Egyptian government was not willing to lose face again. It promptly despatched the head of the EAF, Mahmud Sidki, to Syria on April 10, 1967 so that he and his staff could be fully debriefed on exactly what had occurred during the April 7 clashes. They also had orders to prepare plans to aid the SyAAF should this happen again.

For a while things settled down, but on May 13, 1967 Israeli Intelligence reported that they had received word of the USSR notifying Egypt that the IDF had amassed 13 brigades along the Israeli-Syrian border in preparation for an attack planned for the third week of May. Although there was no truth to the Soviet report, the SyAAF sent a lone MiG-21 on a reconnaissance mission over Israel the following day to photograph the brigades. Egypt also reacted to the supposed Israeli threat by mobilising its forces.

An EAF pilot completes the pre-flight checks of his MiG-21F-13 in 1965. Note that its Arabic serial number, 5172, has been applied with stencils. This seems to have been characteristic of some of the early MiG-21s supplied to Egypt, and might indicate application prior to delivery from the USSR.

Ignoring the emerging crisis, Israel went ahead with its planned Independence Day military march through Jerusalem on May 15 – this event had taken place every year since 1949. Despite its significance, the march was only modest in size because Jerusalem was a divided city (it had been partially controlled by Jordan since 1948) that had been declared a demilitarised zone since 1949. Ignoring Jordanian protests and the condemnation of the UN, Israel staged its Independence Day military march on May 15 as planned. That same day, while he was reviewing the march, Israeli Prime Minister Levy Eshkol was notified that Egyptian armed forces had moved into Sinai.

Israel had not foreseen this move, as the IDF's Intelligence section had not expected Egyptian armed forces to be ready for war before 1968. Unlike the February 1960 crisis, when Egyptian forces mobilised in secret, the Sinai deployment of May 15, 1967 was made very much in the public eye. The next day Egypt demanded the withdrawal of the UNEF, and despite urgent negotiations to diffuse the crisis, the peacekeeping force began leaving Sinai on May 19. Meanwhile, the Israeli government responded to the UN's appeal for calm in the Middle East, indicating its preference to exercise restraint in the face of Egyptian aggression. However, it also warned that a resumption of terrorist activities along its borders or the Egyptian closure of the Straits of Tiran to Israeli shipping would be considered justification for war.

In a show of force, Egypt parachuted a full battalion of troops into Sharem El Sheikh on May 20, 1967. Two days later, President Nasser announced the closure of the Straits of Tiran. Adding insult to injury, during a visit to El Maliz air base he made the immortal statement whilst talking with MiG-21 pilots that if Israel wanted war then "Ahalan WaSahalan" ("welcome"). Concluding that the die was cast in respect to the long-awaited "second round", Israel accepted President Nasser's invitation. Instead of waiting for an Arab attack, Prime Minister Eshkol ordered the IDF/AF to launch a pre-emptive strike on June 5, 1967, thus signalling the start of the Six Day War.

THE COMBATANTS

IDF/AF PILOT TACTICS AND TRAINING

The first IDF/AF unit to operate the Shahak was No. 101 Sqn, its first two examples landing at Hatzor on April 7, 1962 to complete an uneventful ferry flight from France. Deliveries to the second IDF/AF unit to operate the aircraft commenced on July 7, when four arrived at Ramat David to join No. 117 Sqn. Both units were intended to become masters of all trades, as the Shahak was to fly both air-to-air and air-to-ground missions. New weapons and tactics were to be devised and implemented, although these were initially hampered by the Shahak's powerplant and weapons system, which were inferior to equivalent US and UK products. Indeed, no fewer than four Shahaks were lost during 1963 in accidents caused by engine malfunctions, the problem being traced to the Atar 09B's accessory box.

Advertised as a revolutionary fighting machine capable of being operated by a single pilot in all weather conditions, the initial disappointment caused by the Shahak within the IDF/AF was tremendous. It quickly became obvious that the fighter's Mach 2 performance was irrelevant in traditional dogfights, and this was especially true in combat with "inferior" fighters. Although the comparable MiG-21 began to enter EAF service in May 1962, few of the Shahak's opponents in the Middle East fell into the Mach 2 category. They were mostly MiG-17s

and MiG-19s, but also Hunters and, from 1967 onwards, Su-7s as well. The Hunter and the MiG-17 were astonishingly agile, and when Shahak pilots practised their superior-inferior combat tactics against IDF/AF Super Mysteres, it became apparent that they would have to be totally revised so as to ensure that the deltas' supposed superiority would indeed result in defeat for the inferior fighter, and not *vice versa*.

As these adversaries (other than the MiG-19 and Su-7) had superior subsonic turn performance, the emerging Shahak air combat tactics capitalised on the Mach 2 fighter's strengths – its sheer speed, acceleration and rate of climb. The preferred tactic was a sort of "hit and run" pass, which meant using initial GCI vectoring to achieve surprise, preferably from as far away as possible, by the launching of an AAM. The Shahak pilot would close to cannon range only if the AAM missed, which often happened in those days. If he had to dogfight an inferior opponent, the best tactic was to preserve his fighter's higher energy state by climbing or diving, rather than by turning with the enemy, thereby bleeding energy and losing the advantage of speed. To Israeli pilots, the use of the vertical dimension became known as "stitching" because in such conditions a fighter's trajectory in combat often resembled the movement of a hand stitching with needle and thread.

Such tactics took time to evolve and perfect, and their implementation was greatly hampered by the effectiveness of the Shahak's weapons system. Tracing its origins to point defence against bombers equipped with nuclear weapons, the Shahak's weapons system was supposed to incorporate cutting-edge technology. This would have been true if the equipment had worked as advertised, but it rarely did. The CSF Cyrano radar was designed to lock onto a relatively large target flying at high altitude during an interception in which the radar was "looking" upwards. Once lock-on was achieved, the radar-slaved CSF-95 gunsight would acquire the target too, allowing the pilot to quickly take aim and shoot it down from a range of 700 metres. Theoretically, it was a fantastic system, but in reality nothing worked.

In a look-down situation, with the Shahak above the target, the Cyrano was unable to acquire anything below 30,000ft over land – or 10,000ft over the sea – due to ground clutter. Unacceptably low serviceability due in the main to overheating did not inspire confidence in the new system either. In fact, throughout the Shahak's IDF/AF service career only a few air-to-air kills resulted from a proper radar lock-on that had delivered accurate range data to the gunsight. The Cyrano was retained because it was already installed, and nothing else was available. A mid-1960s project to improve Cyrano performance was contracted to Israeli Aircraft Industries Elta, but it had been scrapped by the end of the decade following the delivery of US combat aircraft with superior radar systems. The Cyrano radars were removed shortly thereafter and replaced by a ballast weight.

Different types of aircraft suffer differing levels of vulnerability to battle damage. The MiG-17, the Hunter and the Su-7 could take plenty of punishment, but a single well-placed hit could easily turn a MiG-21 into a spectacular fireball. Air combat tactics in the 1960s dictated three principal phases to achieve a kill, although only the last one was absolutely essential to success. These phases were smart GCI vectoring towards the enemy aircraft to place the fighter in an advantageous position, superior tactics to gain a firing position and the infliction of lethal damage.

No. 101 Sqn Senior Deputy Commander Dan Sever (right) was the first Shahak pilot to engage a MiG-21 in the air during the Six Day War. Having flown Shahaks since April 1963, he was No. 101 Sqn's Senior Deputy Commander from December 1965 until he became its acting CO immediately after the Six Day War – a position he held until November 1967. Sever swapped fighters for airliners when he joined El Al in 1969, although he remained attached to No. 101 Sqn as a reserve pilot from 1970 through to 1980. Sever was credited with 3.5 kills between 1967 and 1973.

IDF/AF GCI tactics were honed to perfection and the Shahak pilots' air combat tactics were of the highest possible standard, but hitting the target remained the key issue. As previously noted, Shahak hit rates with the fighter's 30mm cannon during practice air-to-air gunnery drills were embarrassingly low. Although the build-up of experience on the Shahak and intensive air-to-air gunnery training resulted in constant improvement (up to an average of 22 per cent), there were basic flaws in the system. The Shahaks' inability to shoot down enemy aircraft in at least four air combats between August 1963 and March 1965 certainly highlighted the problem. Pilots did not hit their opponents, and when they did lethal damage was not inflicted. The later problem was easily solved when it was realised that as a bomber interceptor, the Mirage IIIC was firing rounds that were optimised to explode inside a large target. Upon hitting a small tactical fighter the round penetrated, exited and exploded beyond the target, inflicting only light damage rather than ensuring a kill. The obvious cure was to use zero delay-fused rounds that exploded on impact.

No. 101 Sqn groundcrew proudly pose for the photographer both on and around "their" fighter, Shahak 81, which is parked in its hardened aircraft shelter at Hatzor on April 8, 1967. The jet has already been adorned with a kill marking following pilot Avner Slapak's SyAAF MiG-21 kill of the previous day.

YORAM AGMON

Born in Israel during the 1930s, Yoram Agmon commenced his compulsory service in the IDF in the late 1950s as an infantryman. After more than two years "in the trenches", he decided that his future was in the air, and he volunteered for a transfer to the IDF/AF. Agmon graduated as part of Flying School Class 36 on March 12, 1962, his being the final course to go through the full syllabus of primary training in the Stearman biplane, basic training in the Harvard and advanced training in the Meteor.

At that time the Flying School year was divided into three terms, each of which was four months long. These overlapped the Israeli calendar year (April to March). Agmon initially attended the Year 1962 Term 1 (April to July) Ouragan Operational Training Unit (OTU) course, graduates of which were assigned to frontline squadrons. Thanks to his ability as a pilot, Agmon was lucky enough to receive the best posting then available to a new fighter pilot – a Super Mystere squadron. After four terms flying the French fighter, Agmon was assigned to Mirage IIICJ conversion during Year 1963 Term 3 (December to March), and he flew his first mission over the Israeli-Syrian border on November 13, 1964.

In line with the IDF/AF's policy of assigning frontline squadron pilots as flying school instructors, Agmon filled both this role and that of an Emergency Posting Mirage III pilot from December 1964. It was while serving in this dual capacity that Yoram Agmon became the first IDF/AF pilot to be credited with an air-to-air kill (over a MiG-21 from the SyAAF) while flying the Mirage IIICJ on July 14, 1966. The following year he flew 14 missions during the June 1967 Six Day War, but failed to engage enemy aircraft throughout the brief conflict. Agmon did, however, claim his second victory (an EAF Su-7) during post-war clashes on July 15, 1967. In 1969 Agmon's days as a Shahak pilot ended when he undertook F-4 Phantom II conversion in the USA and subsequently served as deputy commander of the first IDF/AF unit to receive the fighter. He flew dozens of missions during the 1969-70 Attrition War, and almost became the first Israeli Phantom II pilot

to be credited with an air-to-air kill but for a malfunction that forced him to give way to his wingman, who duly achieved that claim to fame.

Agmon commanded an A-4 Skyhawk squadron in 1972-73 and an F-4 squadron in 1973-74. It was during the latter posting that he at last achieved ace status when he was credited with three kills during the October 1973 War. Having achieved rare Mirage III/Phantom II ace status, Agmon claimed his sixth, and final, kill during border clashes between Israel and Syria in April 1974. Leaving the F-4 unit later that year, Agmon served as a staff officer and Hatzor wing commander until he retired with the rank of brigadier general in 1982.

Improving aiming required a rather more ingenious solution, and this was provided by the "Shahak Zeroing Team" and its "holding switches", as explained earlier in this volume. Following their introduction, Shahak pilots immediately raised the air-to-air hit rate to 35 per cent. More significantly, Shahaks were credited with 11 gunnery kills in the months that followed. A number of these victories were claimed by Emergency Posting (EP) pilots serving with frontline units. IDF/AF squadrons included four principal categories of aircrew – the management (unit CO and two deputies), regular, EP and reserve. During the early 1960s all aircrew were required to become flying school instructors as part of their career development. They continued to fly with their previous frontline squadrons as EPs, however, serving with the unit for one day a week so as to maintain currency in their fighter type. During exercises, periods of tension and war, EP aircrews were the first to reinforce frontline squadrons, with reserve aircrews only being called up when it was absolutely essential.

ARAB PILOT TACTICS AND TRAINING

In 1959 Israel acquired supersonic Super Mystère jet fighters from France, and the following year the EAF and SyAAF ordered the similarly performing MiG-19 from the Soviet Union. The Middle Eastern arms race was now in full swing. The structure of the EAF throughout this period remained essentially similar to the Royal Air Force, on which it was modelled. A supposed restructuring along Warsaw Pact lines remained superficial, with a wing or *jinaah* simply being renamed an air brigade. Most comprised three squadrons, each with between 15 and 20 aircraft. In the air too, Egyptian pilots used the British tactical "fluid four" formation rather than the tighter Soviet "finger four".

The first group of pilots sent to the USSR to train on the MiG-19 had already flown MiG-17s, and included men who would subsequently become prominent in the EAF. Upon their return, these pilots formed Egypt's first MiG-19 squadron based at Fayid, close to the Suez Canal. President Nasser soon decided that instead of ordering more MiG-19s, Egypt should concentrate on the more advanced MiG-21. Meanwhile, the two MiG-19 squadrons were giving EAF pilots useful experience in operating supersonic fighters.

The first Egyptian pilots to convert to the MiG-21 were veteran squadron leaders or flight lieutenants that had flown the MiG-17 and/or MiG-19, and by 1964 the EAF had about 60 MiG-21F-13s on strength. The first units equipped with the "Fishbed-C" faced a number of early problems. For example, these aircraft were not equipped with a blind landing radio ground control or guidance system. Soviet training was also highly orthodox, influencing Egyptian air tactics and strategy. Interceptions relied on ground-based radars and control to vector pilots to their targets. Such set-piece tactics when combined with limited flying experience clearly reduced the pilots' effectiveness in traditional manoeuvring combat or dogfights. At squadron level, however, the men were confident. Indeed, MiG-21 pilot Kadri el-Hamid made the following comment on Egypt's MiG-21 operations before the June 1967 War:

We used to fly above Israel and do reconnaissance at a height of 18,000 metres. They shot at us with their Hawk missiles, but because of our height they didn't hit us. We were flying over Israeli territory but stayed over it just a short time, so the Mirages couldn't catch us either. None of us thought that we would really fight with Israel, but we felt that we were well prepared should we be called on to do so.

According to Arab air forces historians Dr David Nicolle and Tom Cooper, the SyAAF also initially received 35 to 40 MiG-19Ss prior to taking delivery of the first of its MiG-21F-13s in the early 1960s. Very little is known about the early Syrian service of the MiG-21, as pilot training proved to be relatively slow, and there were considerable equipment problems. The SyAAF also obtained MiG-21FLs (enough for one squadron) and six to eight MiG-21U conversion trainers from 1966.

The MiG-19S was introduced into Iraqi service from 1961, followed by 60 MiG-21F-13s. The first IrAF unit to receive the MiG-21F-13 was the 17th Squadron, which would fly the interceptor for the next 30 years. The IrAF trained intensively with its new MiG-21s, pilots flying 20-22 hours per month, with live-firing air-to-ground exercises every Sunday. Pilots received very little air-to-air gunnery instruction, however.

While their Syrian brethren were trained almost exclusively by Soviet and Egyptian instructors, Iraqi MiG-21 training was undertaken with the help of Indian and British personnel. The training received by new Arab MiG-21 pilots in the USSR was limited to basic flying. The Soviets would not train their Arab customers in navigation, flying at low-level or in the use of MiGs in manoeuvring combat, especially at lower altitudes.

As in Syria, Iraqi crew training was constantly interrupted by political unrest within the armed forces. The IrAF was hit especially hard by purges, losing almost half its pilots. In early February 1963 IrAF Hunters and MiG-21s from Rashid air base bombed the defence ministry building in Baghdad until the dictator, Gen Abdul Karim Kassem, surrendered. The IrAF was on the losing side in the next coup attempt in 1965, however, resulting in even more personnel being purged.

As mentioned earlier, on August 16, 1966 IrAF Capt Munir Radfa took off on a routine training mission but flew his MiG-21F-13 across Jordan to Israel. Radfa's action was planned by Mossad, which had found that the Orthodox Christian pilot was deeply unhappy with the way he was being treated in the IrAF. The affair threw a dark shadow over the air force, especially when some weeks later three more Iraqi pilots defected with their MiG-21s to Jordan. All were granted political asylum, but their aircraft were returned to Iraq.

Once things settled down, Iraq ordered 60 more MiG-21PFs and a few MiG-21US conversion trainers in 1966. They were intended to

This photograph of the defecting IrAF MiG-21F-13 was taken moments after the aircraft had landed at Hatzor on August 16, 1966. Israeli flight-testing soon revealed that the MiG-21's rear hemisphere field of view was appalling, despite its canopy being more "bubble" like than the Mirage IIICJ's.

Contemporary Arab media reports during the period immediately prior to the Six Day War were confident that Egypt and its allies would secure a resounding victory in the "second round" conflict with Israel. Amongst the material published was this May 1967 article in Egyptian magazine *Acher El Saah* following the publication's visit to a MiG-21 squadron "somewhere in Sinai". No. 119 Sqn Shahak pilot Ithamar Neuner translated the photo caption for the author. It read "Our Arab pilots are ready for the moment when they will get to teach Israel a lesson. We will always have the upper hand."

equip four squadrons, but by the spring of 1967 the IrAF still only had two operational MiG-21 units. Initial Iraqi experience with MiG-21s was not, however, particularly positive. The main problems were similar to those faced by other Arab air forces. When the MiG-21 was exported the whole GCI support system that went with the aircraft was rarely purchased, and if it was available it was supplied for the defence of small areas only. Countries like Egypt and Iraq are huge, and the MiG-21s frequently had to operate far beyond the zones covered by GCI stations.

This photograph of an EAF pilot wearing a pressure suit inside the cramped cockpit of a MiG-21F-13 also appeared in the *Acher El Saah* feature of May 1967. Such suits were essential for sorties flown at altitudes in excess of 50,000ft (such as the May-June 1967 overflights of Israel), as they offered the pilot protection from the elements in case of sudden cockpit pressurisation loss due to combat damage or technical malfunction.

NABIL SHOUKRY

Born in Egypt during the 1930s, Nabil Shoukry graduated from the EAF Academy several years after President Nasser had welcomed Soviet military influence in the country. As a young pilot, he initially flew the MiG-17, which was the leading Egyptian fighter in the late 1950s. Having quickly distinguished himself as both a promising fighter pilot and future leader, Shoukry was among the first group of aircrew sent by the EAF to the USSR in June 1960 to convert onto the MiG-19. Shoukry went on to serve in the first squadron to fly the supersonic fighter, his unit being led by future EAF commander Muhammed Alaa El Din Barakat.

By 1967 Shoukry, now a major, was flying the MiG-21FL, and on June 5 he became the first Egyptian "Fishbed" pilot to shoot down an Israeli Mirage IIICJ when he destroyed the No. 101 Sqn aircraft flown by Yair Neuman. He achieved this victory while flying from Inshas, where the EAF's elite interceptor squadrons were traditionally based. Shoukry again engaged Mirage IIICJs on June 8 over Sinai, but he was unable to repeat his success because his MiG-21FL was armed with air-to-ground rocket pods only. Interestingly, Shoukry flew lead during the June 5 engagement over the Nile Delta and as wingman during the air combat over Sinai three days later.

Egypt was involved in several regional conflicts during the 1960s, and shortly after the Six Day War Shoukry was assigned to the EAF deployment to Nigeria. There, he flew MiG-17s primarily in air-to-ground attack missions. During one of these sorties Shoukry claimed to have destroyed a light aeroplane that he had spotted parked near a landing strip, strafing it until it caught fire.

By the time of the Yom Kippur War in October 1973 Shoukry had been promoted to command No. 102 Air Brigade at Inshas. The amount of actual flying done by officers at this level during the conflict varied, but Shoukry led by example, participating in more than one

MiG-21 versus Mirage IIICJ/Nesher engagement. Although he did not claim any more aerial victories, Shoukry claimed that his section shot down four Mirage IIICJs or Neshers for the loss of a solitary MiG-21. The latter report may well be accurate but the former claim is certainly not, since the IDF/AF never lost four delta fighters in a single combat.

Shoukry eventually attained the rank of major general, and was EAF Chief of Operations in 1990. He played a prominent part in peace talks between Egypt and Israel in the late 1970s, and after one such meeting between high ranking military officers from both sides Shoukry mentioned his Six Day War kill to Israeli Minister of Defence Ezer Weizman. Intrigued, Weizman ordered Giora Romm — a Mirage IIICJ pilot during this period, as well as the IDF/AF's first ace — to check the accuracy of Shoukry's claim. Romm duly researched the action of June 5 prior to meeting Shoukry in person to hear his story. After the two veteran fighter pilots had finally parted, Romm subsequently reported to Weizman that he had indeed met the man who had shot down Yair Neuman.

COMBAT

The first encounter between the Middle East's Mach 2 fighters took place on July 19, 1964. That day, No. 119 Sqn Shahaks had photographed 24 EAF MiG-21s parked in three lines and ten more jets in a large pen, possibly stored, at Cairo West. A handful of Egyptian "Fishbed-Cs" were scrambled to intercept the two reconnaissance Shahaks, but by then the latter aircraft were already heading for home at high speed. Nevertheless, during the pursuit one of the MiG-21s closed to within 3.5 miles of the IDF/AF fighters and launched an "Atoll" AAM. The latter had been fired at the very limit of its range in a tail chase scenario and the weapon fell behind the Shahaks. The two Israeli jets returned to Tel Nof minus their external fuel tanks, which had been jettisoned during ingress as planned. The Egyptian army recovered the wreckage of the empty tanks and used them as evidence to back up EAF claims that the intruding Israeli fighters had been shot down.

The first actual engagement between Shahaks and MiG-21s occurred four months later on November 14, 1964. Activity started at 1330 hrs when an IDF/AF Vautour, escorted by No. 117 Sqn Shahaks, flew a reconnaissance mission over Syria. Four SyAAF MiG-21s were scrambled too late to intercept the formation. The Vautour returned home after completing its photo runs, but a second Shahak Combat Air Patrol (CAP) remained over Syria to cover its egress. At 1510 hrs IDF/AF Intelligence detected four more SyAAF MiG-21s taking off, and five minutes later Israeli GCI started to track two Syrian "Fishbed-Cs" flying west at 22,000ft.

By now the two Shahaks manning the CAP were from No. 101 Sqn, operating with the call-sign "Heavy". GCI vectored them into position for a perfect head-on interception, but "Heavy 1", flown by future ace Amos Amir, was unable to achieve radar lock-on. At a range of three miles he abandoned the radar lock option and started to visually look for the MiG-21s. By then the latter were flying straight and

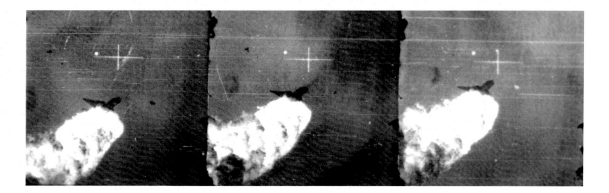

level at 23,000ft over Syrian territory, with the Shahaks slightly below them at 20,000ft. Just as the pairs started to cross each other's flight paths, the No. 101 Sqn jets jettisoned their external fuel tanks and initiated a right-hand turn while accelerating and climbing. The MiG-21s, possibly still unaware of the Shahaks' presence, turned through 180 degrees so as to avoid crossing the Israeli-Syrian border.

Having gone supersonic, "Heavy 1" had closed the gap on the trailing MiG-21 to 1,200 metres, at which point he fired a Shafrir AAM. The SyAAF pilot continued to fly straight and level in afterburner, thus making an ideal target for an infrared-homing missile. The Shafrir launch sequence was perfectly executed, but instead of homing onto the aircraft's hot jet pipe, the missile dived into the ground! "Heavy 1", continuing to follow the MiG-21, opted for cannon instead and selected the manual override range of 400 metres prior to opening fire. His first burst missed, but rounds from the second burst hit the MiG-21. They had no effect on their target, however.

After four minutes of combat, IDF/AF GCI ordered "Heavy" to disengage. The two Shahaks turned west, followed by the MiG-21 leader, who launched an AAM against "Heavy 1". The "Atoll", which was only marginally more advanced than the Shafrir in terms of its guidance technology, also missed.

During the course of this engagement all Shahak air-to-air weapons had failed in actual combat. The Yahalom could not be launched without radar lock, the Shafrir failed to guide and the gun rounds failed to shoot the MiG-21 down, despite them clearly hitting their target. The analysis of the cannon failure concluded that the rounds were equipped with delay-fused detonators optimised for the interception of bombers. When used against smaller fighters, the rounds penetrated and exited prior to them exploding, so damage to the MiG-21 was not fatal. They were immediately replaced with impact-detonated rounds.

The lack of Syrian success in this action was probably due to shortcomings in the SyAAF's GCI network. The MiG-21 pilots seemed to be totally unaware of the Shahaks' presence until "Heavy 1" opened fire with his 30mm cannon. And because the Syrian pilots were ignorant of the danger that they were in, neither of them jettisoned their fuel tanks or manoeuvred aggressively. However, from the moment "Heavy" flight was exposed after being ordered back to Israel, the lead MiG-21 pilot chose to go after the disengaging Shahaks and attempt an "Atoll" attack, rather than immediately escorting his wingman's damaged jet home.

Shahak pilots quickly discovered that the MiG-21 typically burst into flames when hit by 30mm cannon rounds. As this gunsight camera view taken during the Six Day War clearly reveals, the proximity of a high-octane fuel tank to an oxygen bottle in the "Fishbed's" centre fuselage usually caused the jet to erupt in a fireball of flames when it was struck in this area by cannon rounds. The IDF/AF evaluation of the ex-IrAF MiG-21 had highlighted this potentially deadly design flaw to all Shahak pilots.

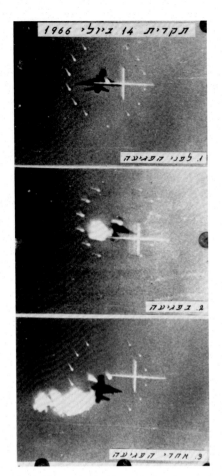

הקרבה 14 בנולי 1966

1. לפני הפגיעה

2. הפגיעה

3. אחרי הפגיעה

These three frames from the gunsight camera of Shahak 59 were taken on July 14, 1966 when Yoram Agmon claimed the French fighter's first aerial kill. The first one in the sequence was taken prior to the pilot opening fire, and it reveals that his aiming point was the starboard wing root of the Syrian jet – his rounds actually hit the port wing root, however. The second frame is blurred due to the shuddering of the Shahak as Agmon opens fire. The final frame shows the damaged MiG-21 trailing flames, as well as a secondary fire just behind the cockpit, which could possibly be the start of the ejection seat sequence.

The next clash to take place came about due to an increase in hostilities associated with the Water War. On July 14, 1966, as part of Operation *Wind*, the IDF/AF was tasked with attacking Syrian engineering vehicles from 1600 hrs. Among the support elements for the fighter-bombers were two four-ship Shahak CAP formations. At H-Hour the No. 119 Sqn CAP commenced flying a racetrack pattern at 15,000ft well inside Syrian territory in an effort to block incoming SyAAF interceptors. No. 101 Sqn's back-up CAP set up its racetrack pattern at 25,000ft over Israeli territory, just west of the border. The air strike was over and the frontline CAP had withdrawn by the time four MiG-21s were scrambled from Dmer at 1623 hrs and vectored towards the Israeli-Syrian border. Israeli GCI tracked the jets as they split into two pairs and headed west. Yoram Agmon recalled:

We returned from lunch and there was a four-ship formation planned for a CAP, but the pilot scheduled to fly as No 4 had to go somewhere so I took his place. We relieved another CAP and were patrolling along the Golan Heights on our side of the border when GCI ordered "full power west". I knew that igniting the afterburner whilst the jet was still equipped with large external tanks only wasted fuel, as the aircraft would achieve roughly the same speed without reheat. Maybe I would lag behind a little, but as No 4 I was entitled to, so I was the only one who did not fly with afterburner. Then GCI ordered us to turn east, by which point I already had about 300-400 litres more fuel than the others. As we headed east I observed two MiGs at low altitude – we were flying at 20,000ft. I reported seeing them, lowered my nose and jettisoned the external tanks. I tried very hard not to lose sight of them against the cluttered backdrop of the landscape below because they were only tiny dots. They soon disappeared from my view, however. It was at this point that I decided to dive to the lowest altitude I could and acquire them by looking up in the same direction above the horizon. That's exactly what happened.

As I levelled out I saw them about two kilometres ahead of me. When I was behind them – not yet within range to open fire with my cannon – and at low altitude, there was no AAM option. They broke hard, someone having possibly warned them. Their break surprised me, as it was a beautiful turn, a great break, but it gave me the opportunity to close the distance on them. I was now in a position to open fire on the leading MiG. The trailing MiG was still in the area but not in the picture, and he probably never saw me. I opened fire but missed. My second or third burst hit the wing and the jet immediately spun in and exploded. The pilot ejected and I saw his empty cockpit. I then watched the MiG crash.

The action had happened at an altitude of about 500ft. The other pilots landed at Ramat David due to a shortage of fuel, but I was able to fly to Hatzor, where there was great joy. I don't know if it's true, but the groundcrew counted the cannon rounds upon my return to base and told me that I had expended exactly 101!

46

MIRAGE IIICJ COCKPIT

1. CSF-95 gunsight
2. Instrument panel UV lights
3. Angle-of-attack (AOA) indicator
4. SEPR 84 rocket motor control
5. Aircraft/radar heading indicator
6. Malfunctions panel
7. Electrical load reduction switches
8. Condensation removal lever
9. G meter
10. Altimeter
11. Fire warning lights
12. Indicated airspeed and mach meter
13. Attitude director indicator (ADI)
14. Radio compass heading indicator
15. Hydraulic pressure selector
16. Hydraulic pressure indicator

17. Canopy lock
18. Canopy ejection handle
19. Emergency artificial horizon
20. Vertical speed indicator (VSI)
21. "Mice" variable engine inlet mach indicator
22. Cyrano CSF radar scope
23. Jet nozzle temperature
24. Fuel transfer indicator
25. Afterburner control (switch for emergency activation, left light fuel injection, right light afterburner ON)
26. Engine RPM
27. Fuel gauge
28. Parking brake lever and indicator light
29. Radio compass control panel
30. Exterior lights switch
31. Landing gear lever

32. "Mice" variable inlet control switches (auto/manual)
33. Jettison panel (three switches from left to right – fuselage station, wing stations and external fuel tanks)
34. Rudder pedals
35. Control column
36. Cockpit depressurisation/ram-air lever
37. Throttle
38. UHF 1 radio control panel
39. Weapons panel
40. Condensation removal switch
41. Radar control handle
42. UHF 2 radio control dial
43. Missile selector
44. Seat adjustment lever
45. Torch
46. IFF control panel

47. Fuel control panel for engine and afterburner
48. Pilot's seat
49. Circuit breaker panel
50. Arm rest
51. Clock
52. Standby compass
53. Weapons panel
54. Warning light for non-extended landing gear
55. Mach limit warning light
56. Missile selection indicators
57. Drag chute release handle
58. Map compartments
59. Landing gear indicator lights
60. Emergency landing gear extension lever
61. Fuel jettison switch
62. Ejection handle
63. Gunsight selector switch

These three gunsight camera frames from Shahak 60 show the view that pilot Avi Lanir had on April 7, 1967. Having tracked his prey he opened fire, causing the Syrian MiG-21 to blow up directly in front of him. Miraculously, Lanir's Shahak emerged intact and made it home to Ramat David.

7 אפריל 1967

לפני הפגיעה

בפגיעה

אחרי הפגיעה

Yoram Agmon's historic kill was confirmed by his gun camera film, which showed the MiG-21 on fire and the Syrian pilot ejecting. The subsequent crash was also witnessed by at least two Israeli pilots.

Water War fighting was, in the main, triggered by a pre-planned operation that either side had initiated. However, a few of the large-scale clashes during this period came about due to the escalation of a local skirmish. The most famous of these came on April 7, 1967 when an exchange of artillery fire between Israel and Syria provoked a fully blown tank and air battle that saw six SyAAF MiG-21s downed, while the IDF/AF suffered no losses. As these results confirm, the Israelis made the most of their numerical superiority on this date, dominating Syrian skies through the launching of 171 sorties compared with only 34 by the SyAAF. Most of the IDF/AF sorties saw fighter-bombers conducting air-to-ground missions, while most of the Syrian missions were defensive air-to-air in nature. Despite the SyAAF concentrating on the latter, the IDF/AF still enjoyed numerical superiority with 52 Shahak CAP sorties being generated versus only 28 by the MiG-21 force.

Despite the number of fighters in the sky during the course of the day, only four engagements took place. The first started at 1358 hrs when Israeli GCI placed a pair of No. 101 Sqn aircraft in a perfect position behind two MiG-21s patrolling over Damascus. Mistakenly believing that they were safe flying over their own capital, the two Syrians pilots were unaware of the Shahaks' presence until too late. Lead pilot and future ace Iftach Spector opened fire, but he was closing too fast on his target and his first burst missed. To avoid overtaking the MiG-21 Spector pulled abruptly up into a climb, flew over the aircraft and then slipped back into its "six o'clock" position. His burst of cannon fire hit the MiG-21 hard, after which Spector pulled up again.

Meanwhile, wingman Beni Romach was doing well against the trailing MiG-21, gradually closing on it until he opened fire from a distance of 400 metres. The SyAAF fighter was definitely damaged, but at this point Spector ordered his wingman to turn away. Romach obeyed and his leader locked his Cyrano onto the damaged MiG-21 and launched his Yahalom at it. The latter exploded in front of the Shahak, so Spector switched to cannon, opened fire and finished off the MiG-21.

During the nine engagements between the MiG-21 and the Mirage IIICJ from July 1964 to April 1967, the latter had claimed eight kills in five combats. Six of these victories were definitely confirmed by reports of the pilot ejecting or the aircraft being seen to crash. All eight kills were credited to cannon fire, despite Shahak pilots launching a Yahalom and no fewer than seven Shafrirs. Arab pilots had, in return, fired two "Atoll" AAMs. All ten missiles had failed to find their targets.

Most of these engagements demonstrated the clear superiority of the IDF/AF's GCI system. Shahak pilots were vectored into perfect firing positions directly behind enemy MiG-21s on six occasions, and in five of these kills were claimed. All of these successful combats were exclusively tail chase interceptions that were over before they could evolve into dogfights. Shahak pilots reported that only twice did their MiG-21 opponents turn in an effort to break away from tail chase attack profiles. In both engagements, the MiG-21 break (steep in the first and gentle in the second) did not change the outcome. In fact they only served the attacker's objective, as the turns

No. 117 Sqn personnel gather round the blackened Shahak 60 on the taxiway of its hardened aircraft shelter at Ramat David. Avi Lanir had to endure poor visibility from the cockpit for the remainder of the flight as his windscreen and canopy were both liberally covered in soot.

slowed down their fighters, thus enabling the Shahak pilots to rapidly close the distance to effective cannon range.

Although the April 7 combat was the last fighter clash prior to the Six Day War, the escalation towards all out conflict accelerated on May 14 when a Syrian MiG-21 flew a reconnaissance mission over Israel. Similar sorties by EAF MiG-21s followed from May 17, contemporary Israeli evaluation of these incursions referring to them as "hostile reconnaissance flights". Israeli GCI had tracked high-altitude, high-speed MiG-21 reconnaissance training flights over Egypt from late 1966, IDF/AF Intelligence monitoring their radio transmissions. The flights prompted Shahak pilots to refresh their interception skills against "high and fast" targets. Indeed, IDF/AF Weapon Systems Section test pilot Ezra Aharon flew four high-altitude (58,000ft to 62,500ft) sorties from November 27 to simulate the expected Arab MiG-21 flight profile for the benefit of fellow Shahak pilots who were practising interceptions.

Israeli Mirage IIICJs also occasionally flew over Sinai during this period too as they tested EAF reaction times to their incursions – the latter were often made at low-level. These provocative sorties prompted a spur of the moment flight by unit commander and early Egyptian MiG-21 pilot Fuad Kamal, as he recalled:

A No. 101 Sqn Shahak shoots down a Syrian MiG-21 on April 7, 1967.

MiG-21F-13 COCKPIT

1. Oxygen controls
2. Rocket/cannon arming switch
3. Flap controls
4. Seat height adjustment switch
5. Navigation lights switch
6. Throttle, with controls for radio, airbrake and target radar range
7. Air start switch
8. Anti-surge valves switch
9. Nose cone manual/auto operation
10. Hydraulic pump switches
11. K-18 oxygen gauge
12. Landing gear lever
13. Landing gear position indicator

14. UD-1 range indicator
15. Brake overheating lights
16. V-1 voltmeter
17. Accelerometer
18. Landing light switch
19. External tank jettison switch
20. ARU-3? automatic control
21. Air speed indicator
22. Compass
23. Radio switch
24. Trim control
25. Gun/radar sight
26. Attitude indicator
27. Altimeter
28. Clock

29. Cannon indicator lights
30. Rate-of-climb inidicator
31. Landing gear warning light
32. Trim/stabiliser warning lights
33. Emergency pitot tube switches
34. Turn and bank indicator
35. Missile control panel
36. Mach meter
37. Tachometer
38. Exhaust gas temperature gauge
39. Fuel tank pump switches
40. Fuel flow meter
41. Control column

42. Tyre pressure gauge
43. Fuses
44. KM-1 ejection seat
45. Rudder pedals
46. Radio altimeter
47. Hydraulic pressure gauge
48. Angle-of-attack indicator
49. Pressure gauge for emergency systems
50. Cockpit lighting
51. Radio control panel
52. Main selector switches for missiles, radar, external stores, avionics, nose-cone systems
53. IFF code selector

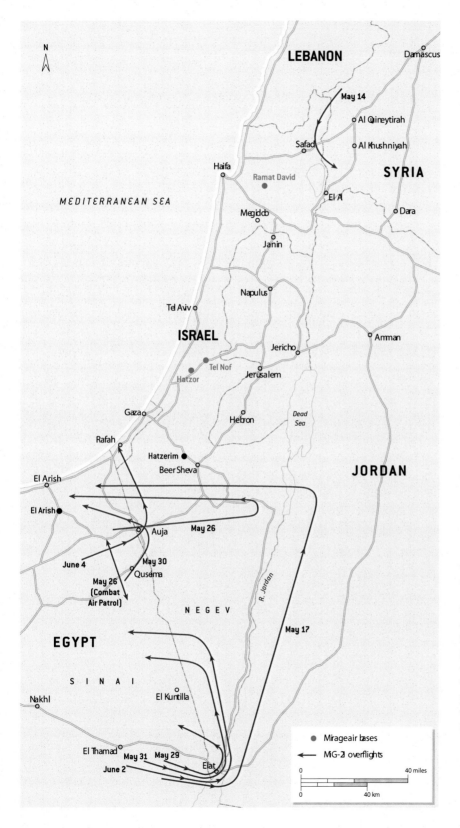

N

LEBANON

Damascus

May 14

○ Al Quneytirah

Safad ○

○ Al Khushniyah

Haifa ○

Ramat David ●

SYRIA

MEDITERRANEAN SEA

○ El Al

Megiddo ○

○ Dara

Janin ○

Napulus ○

Tel Aviv ○

ISRAEL

Jericho ○

○ Amman

Tel Nof ●

Hatzor ●

Jerusalem ○

Gaza ○

Hebron ○

Dead Sea

Rafah ○

Hatzerim ●

Beer Sheva ○

JORDAN

El Arish ○

El Arish ●

Auja ●

May 26

R. Jordan

June 4

May 30

Qusema

May 26
(Combat Air Patrol)

NEGEV

May 17

EGYPT

S I N A I

El Kuntilla ○

Nakhl ○

El Thamad ○ **May 31** **May 29**

June 2 Elat ○

● Mirage air bases

← MiG-21 overflights

0 — 40 miles

0 — 40 km

Arab MiG-21s made a series of reconnaissance overflights of Israel between May 14 and June 4, 1967. The first was performed by a Syrian aircraft that supposedly "verified" what ultimately proved to be a false Soviet intelligence report claiming mechanised troops of the IDF were massing along the Israeli-Syrian border. The seven EAF overflights that followed from May 17 further heightened the tension in the region prior to the eruption of the Six Day War. Three of the overflights (May 14 and 30 and June 4) were relatively minor incursions in terms of their duration and distance covered, while those on May 29 and 31 and June 2 covered the southern Negev in search of IDF forces conducting diversionary manoeuvres. Only two missions (May 17 and 26) ventured well into Israeli airspace, heading as far east as Dimona. These overflights quickly revealed that the IDF/AF was virtually powerless to stop the high-flying MiG-21s, although it could be argued that the Israelis had no interest in intercepting the three southern Negev missions in any case. Only the two Dimona missions gave Shahak pilots a remote chance of downing the intruders, and even then the limited time that the EAF jets were over Israel combined with the Mirage IIICJ's poor performance at high altitude to prevent the MiG-21s from being intercepted.

Three of the EAF's first MiG-21 pilots are seen in pressure suits in 1964. The man in the middle is believed to be Fuad Kamal, who led a squadron made up of surviving MiG-21s after the initial Israeli assault on June 5, 1967.

One evening I was out on the tarmac at Abu Sueir when two Israeli aircraft made a low-level pass at dusk. They were too low for our radar to pick them up, so we had had no warning that they were heading for us. My pilots were furious, and they couldn't understand how such a thing could happen. I told them that to undertake such a flight was easy, and to prove it I decided to do the selfsame thing. I took off, crossed the frontier and flew north-northeast at low-level. I flew a circuit, going right over the Israeli flying school, where I saw training aircraft in the circuit. I went as far as Haifa, at which point my jet's fuel light started to flicker, so I turned towards the coast before heading home at very low altitude along the beach, filming anything interesting along the way.

Fellow Egyptian MiG-21 pilot Kadri el-Hamid of No 45 Sqn, which was based at El Maliz, participated in the pre-planned reconnaissance flights in the spring of 1967:

We used to fly over Israel at an altitude of around 18,000 metres. They shot at us with their Hawk SAMs but the weapons could not reach our height. Nevertheless, we stayed over Israeli territory just long enough to get the mission done so that the Mirage IIIs couldn't catch us either.

As Kadri el-Hamid alluded to, Egyptian flights over Israel were brief in their duration. In fact the track of the longest incursion was just 100 miles – a MiG-21 flying at Mach 1.5+ covered this distance in less than six minutes. A clean Shahak, flying a minimum time to altitude profile in ideal weather conditions, was expected to reach 50,000ft just five minutes after take off, at which point the fighter was flying at Mach 1.3 some 40 miles from base. The time it took the pilot to run to the jet and take off also had to be factored in, as had the often less than ideal atmospheric conditions in the region, especially in the hot and humid summer months.

Once aloft, the pilot had 1.5 minutes to accelerate from Mach 0.9 to Mach 1.5+ in full afterburner, reaching the latter speed at 36,000ft. Positioning himself for the attack took still more time, as he had to be directly behind the enemy aircraft so as to ensure the best possible firing resolution for the Shahak's less than reliable AAMs – the preferred weapon in such an engagement. Prior to getting to this point, the pilot would have had to jettison his external tanks and then closely manage the consumption of his remaining fuel reserves, prior to closing in on the MiG-21s while still climbing. All of this had to take place in just a matter of moments, as the "Fishbeds" usually stayed in Israeli airspace for less than six minutes.

One of those to see the high-flying MiG-21s was future ranking Israeli ace Giora Epstein, who recalled:

I converted to the Shahak in August 1966 and achieved air-to-air operational qualification in April 1967. My encounter with an EAF reconnaissance MiG-21 occurred on one of my first QRA scrambles. We were the second QRA pair to take-off, scrambling just minutes after the first had launched. GCI reported MiG-21s flying from west to east, so we jettisoned our external tanks shortly after take-off and climbed as fast as we could. My leader was David Ivry and his Shahak was armed with Yahalom and Shafrir missiles. My jet was fitted with a Yahalom only, which in turn meant that it produced less drag and climbed faster, so I was quickly ahead of my leader.

We saw the MiG-21s "sky-writing" – producing white condensation vapour trails – ahead of us, but we were too low to bother them and they continued flying east. We were still climbing when they turned west again towards El Arish. By then our tactic had changed into an "overtaking interception". We were supposed to settle into a position ahead of them and wait for them to overtake us. I flew south, climbing through 43,000ft and accelerating close to Mach 1. Ivry told me that I too was "sky-writing", but I ignored this and focused my attention on the MiG-21s. They were right in front of me, but at a higher altitude and flying much faster. I waited for the right moment and started to turn west so that when they overtook me, I would be right behind them.

I actually saw my foes – two MiG-21s – flying very close to each other in typical

Ranking Israeli ace Giora Epstein is seen here sat in the cockpit of No. 101 Sqn's Shahak 51. A Mirage IIICJ pilot from 1966 until 1982, he claimed 17 victories between 1967 and 1973, including nine MiG-21s.

Egyptian fashion at 50,000ft. I locked-on my radar, which was quite a rare achievement for the Cyrano, and saw a blue light in the cockpit which indicated that the Yahalom was ready for launch. But I was a novice fighter pilot and made an error – I asked permission to open fire! Before Ivry had had the chance to grant my request GCI told me not to open fire. I didn't understand why, so I again asked my leader for permission to open fire, which was firmly denied by GCI.

At around this time the two MiG-21 pilots switched off their afterburners and started to descend as they neared the Egyptian border and their base at El Arish. They descended through my altitude and I started to close in on them, at which point GCI ordered us to disengage and immediately turn north. I am sure that had I not received this order I would have been able to close in on both MiGs and shoot them down with my cannon. We disengaged and turned north as instructed.

It was only during our subsequent debrief that we realised GCI had confused us and the first QRA pair that was vectored to intercept two EAF MiG-21s that had flown south as decoys for the main reconnaissance mission. Just as I had asked permission to open fire, the first QRA pair had crossed the border into the demilitarised airspace over Sinai. GCI had made a real mess of the interceptions, thinking that the first QRA pair was asking permission to open fire as it crossed the border, and not realising that it was the second QRA pair that had the EAF jets in their gunsights while still flying over our territory. GCI apologised during the debrief, but our opportunity had gone.

Although Israeli GCI would scramble Shahaks long before the MiG-21s actually crossed the border, even this head start failed to bring the Egyptian fighters within weapons range. While IDF/AF planners and pilots strived to find a solution to this problem, an alternative fighter was proposed for the job. As previously mentioned in this book, the MiG-21 was clearly superior to the Mirage III in the vertical fight thanks to its better thrust-to-weight ratio. Although the latter aircraft was the standard IDF/AF QRA jet, the Israelis also possessed the ex-IrAF MiG-21F-13 that had defected in August 1966. Anxious to deter such overflights, the IDF/AF duly modified the aircraft so that it could both carry and launch combat-capable test examples of the new Shafrir 2 AAM. The "Fishbed-C" was also painted in a conspicuous scheme to minimise the risk of a 'friendly fire' incident and parked in readiness within the No. 101 Sqn QRA complex at Hatzor. Preparations for combat missions in the jet were completed in early June 1967, but the scramble never came as Egyptian MiG-21 reconnaissance flights gave way to full-scale war.

The Six Day War commenced with a pre-emptive strike against Egyptian military targets by the IDF/AF on the morning of June 5, 1967. At the time EAF MiG-21s were located at five air bases – El Maliz, in Sinai, to where a MiG-21 squadron had deployed from May 17, Abu Sueir and Fayid in the Suez Canal Zone, Inshas in the Nile Delta and Cairo West.

The question of why no MiG-21s were in the air at the time of the Israeli assault has never been adequately answered. Egyptian MiGs had been flying standing patrols throughout daylight hours, but these were ended on the evening of June 3. Instead, there were only dawn patrols (and a manned QRA), as the EAF expected a traditional attack by the IDF/AF at this time. These missions usually ended shortly after 0700 hrs, so there were no MiG-21s in the air when Israeli combat aircraft struck ten Egyptian airfields.

The first wave of IDF/AF jets took off from their bases at around 0800 hrs Egyptian time, and they started attacking the EAF's key MiG-21 bases 45 minutes later. The Israeli aircraft crossed the border into Sinai at extremely low altitude and technicians manning radar systems saw nothing. As a result, the EAF's interceptor bases were caught entirely by surprise.

A total of 60 Shahaks participated in the first wave of the Israeli pre-emptive strike, with 12 jets divided into six pairs manning QRAs, 45 tasked with attacking five airfields and three flying escort or reconnaissance missions. The Shahaks attacked three MiG-21 bases (Abu Sueir, Cairo West and Inshas), and two of the 12 air base attack formations did not fly the briefed drill of one bombing run against the runways and three strafing passes against parked aircraft. The two exceptions only bombed the runways, after which they flew CAPs over Sinai and the Suez Canal Zone protecting less capable IDF/AF aircraft from EAF MiG-21s. One of these two CAPs subsequently provided the first Shahak versus "Fishbed" aerial engagement of the Six Day War.

Only a handful of QRA MiG-21s made it off from damaged runways, and those that did were quickly engaged by prowling IDF/AF fighters. One such aircraft

ENGAGING THE ENEMY

The Mirage IIICJ's two principal aiming instruments were the radar screen and the CSF-95 lead computing optical gunsight. For the pilot to achieve a radar lock onto a target, he had to move his left hand from the throttle to the radar handle. A switch on the latter locked the radar onto the contact and a blue light flashed in the cockpit if a successful lock-on was achieved. Lock-on, blue light and an audible headset tone were the prerequisites prior to the launching of a semi-active radar-homing Yahalom AAM. In order for this weapon to hit its target, the pilot had to maintain a continuous radar lock-on, since the missile homed onto the target's radar returns. This meant that the Shahak had to "follow" the AAM from launch to impact.

When it came to operating the CSF-95 gunsight, the pilot had a choice of two principal modes – air-to-air and air-to-ground. Air-to-air options were missiles, rockets and cannon. The key gunsight elements appeared in yellow-green, the most dominant of which was the cross, which represented the longitudinal axis of the aircraft. The two dynamic elements of the gunsight were its projected pipper and ring of diamonds. The pipper was the air-to-air aiming point, and its position, relative to the cross, represented lead computed deflection for accurate gunfire, regardless of gravity and manoeuvre. The pipper diameter was two milliradians (representing a two-foot circle at a distance of 1,000 yards), while each of the diamonds in the projected ring measured one milliradian. The radius of the diamond ring represented range. When the radar was locked on, the ring radius constantly changed to reflect radar range measurements.

The pilot had to place the pipper on the target and open fire when the diameter of the diamond ring matched the dimensions of the enemy aircraft.

When the gunsight was in manual override mode, the pilot had to input the target's wingspan through a special knob on the left side of the gunsight. He then had to estimate its range and feed this figure into the CSF-95 via two switches on the underside of the throttle. The switch immediately beneath his index finger selected close range (250 metres), the middle switch closest to his ring finger selected medium range (400 metres) and the activation of both switches saw long range (600 metres) selected. Once the range had been chosen and the gunsight configured, the diameter of the diamond ring remained fixed. The pilot then had to place the pipper on the target once again and match its wingspan to the diameter of the diamond ring.

scrambled from El Maliz soon ran into a three-jet No. 101 Sqn CAP that had just bombed Bir Tamada. Leading the Israeli fighters was Dan Sever:

> Having attacked the runway with our 500kg bombs, we pulled up and flew north past pillars of black smoke rising from nearby Bir Gafgafa (El Maliz) air base. As I looked over in that direction I spotted an Il-14 flying slowly at about 3000ft. I reported this to my Nos 2 and 3 and then dived at the transport at full speed. When I was still several kilometres away I saw a MiG-21 turning east. Switching targets, I reported this to my wingmen and then got organised for the kill. As I closed to within 600 metres of the fighter, and just as I was getting ready to squeeze the trigger, it entered a spin. The aircraft made two complete turns and then crashed.

This was the first recorded MiG-21 versus Mirage III "no weapon" kill – an aircraft flown into the ground during combat. At first, the IDF/AF did not count such claims as legitimate kills. Later on, most of "no weapon" kills were classified as "squadron victories", but some were credited to pilots who had threatened the enemy aircraft and caused it to crash. Interestingly, this ambiguous attitude towards such claims lasted from 1967 until 1982, when the IDF/AF introduced the title "manoeuvre kill".

These early clashes highlighted the major drawback of the "Fishbed" – its chronic lack of firepower. As previously noted, the MiG-21FL was armed with just two unreliable AAMs, while the MiG-21F-13 boasted an identical missile load-out and a single 30mm cannon that had a limited supply of ammunition. A number of Israeli Six Day War fighter-bomber pilots reported being chased by MiG-21s that inexplicably did not open fire on them, and this may well have been because they had already exhausted their AAMs and/or their precious few cannon rounds.

The IDF/AF was well aware of the MiG-21's shortcomings in respect to the jet's armament, and in the main its pilots generally ignored Egyptian MiG-21s on June 5. However, over Abu Sueir, Israeli reports indicated that between ten and twenty "Fishbeds" defended the airfield during the first wave attack – this may well have been a cumulative total, with multiple sightings made of the same aircraft.

Operating with the radio call-sign "Fence", future aces Eitan Karmi ("Fence 1") and Giora Romm ("Fence 2") of No. 119 Sqn had scrambled at 0848 hrs for an offensive fighter sweep of the MiG base. Arriving overhead Abu Sueir at around 0910 hrs, "Fence 2" spotted a MiG-21 taking off from a taxiway and positioned his Shahak for an attack. However, "Fence 1" ordered his wingman to break off his attack so that he could in turn launch a Shafrir at the MiG. The AAM missed, so Karmi switched to cannons instead. The first burst missed the EAF fighter, but the second sent the MiG-21 crashing to the ground. By then "Fence 2" had switched his attention to a second MiG-21, and he eventually claimed two "Fishbeds" destroyed. Romm was also credited with a second MiG-21 kill too.

Within roughly two hours of the Six Day War commencing, the IDF/AF had claimed the destruction of nearly 200 Egyptian aircraft. Israel had achieved air superiority, thus changing the balance of power in the Middle East. Israeli Intelligence reported at 1030 hrs that of the five Egyptian MiG-21 bases, only Abu Sueir and

Inshas remained operational. It also stated that "one MiG-21 shot down another MiG-21, after which it too was subsequently shot down by Egyptian AAA fire". Aside from these losses, the IDF/AF claimed "about ten MiG-21s shot down" and "some 55 destroyed on the ground by strafing". The EAF's force of 102 MiG-21s had been reduced to 37 aircraft in the space of just two hours, giving the IDF/AF numerical supremacy in the skies over the Sinai Desert. These figures are based on Israeli data for Shahak losses and estimated victory claims. Regrettably, accurate Arab figures to corroborate this information is unavailable.

Some four hours after the IDF/AF's pre-emptive strike had been launched at 0745 hrs, Syrian fighter-bombers, escorted by MiG-21s, launched an offensive against Israeli targets. The IDF/AF's fighter force was ordered to both attack Syrian air bases and defend Israel from intruding SyAAF fighter-bombers. A total of four Syrian MiG-21s fell to Shahaks on June 5, although one of the early clashes also resulted in the destruction of a No. 117 Sqn fighter when pilot Ehud Henkin opened fire at such close range to his target that debris from the exploding "Fishbed" fatally damaged the Israeli aircraft. Henkin successfully ejected from his stricken fighter near Ramat David air base.

The tempo of air strikes against Egyptian air bases slowed down as the day progressed, the IDF/AF having essentially achieved its objective of air superiority during the morning missions. The focus of attention for the Shahak units now shifted to air bases in Syria and Jordan. No longer being routinely bombed and strafed, groundcrews at Inshas managed to get three MiG-21FLs and a MiG-21F-13 serviceable. Having found a 900-metre-long section of intact runway, the four "Fishbeds" took-off to fly CAP over the Nile Delta some two hours after Inshas had first been attacked. At the controls of one of those aircraft was Nabil Shoukry:

I initially flew a CAP over Bilbays before my base told me that there were Mirages over Inshas. Racing home, I saw two Mirages to the left of me. I came in behind them until I saw the wingman's helmet. I was just looking because I couldn't shoot due to the limitations of my "Atoll" missile – my MiG-21FL carried two AAMs only. The Mirages dived away and ran for the border, which gave me a chance to shoot at least one of them down. I followed them and fired an "Atoll" at the leader. The first missile hit and there was heavy smoke. I looked for the wingman but didn't see him, so I decided to launch a second missile at the aircraft. The Mirage exploded, pitching up in a stall turn and then the nose fell away.

Shoukry had engaged two Shahaks from a No. 101 Sqn four-aircraft formation that was operating with the call-sign "Chair". Having taken off from Hatzor at 1225 hrs, the jets had performed an attack on Cairo West and then become separated as they headed for home. The leader of the trailing pair inconclusively engaged a MiG-21 prior to returning to Hatzor after his wingman – the latter had lost his leader shortly after attacking Cairo West. The leading pair, meanwhile, possibly remained together, but wingman Yair Neuman was indeed shot down. Shoukry was almost certainly responsible for "Chair 2's" loss, despite him claiming to have shot

Yair Neuman had the unfortunate distinction of being the only Shahak pilot to officially fall victim to an EAF MiG-21 in the Six Day War. Having earned his IDF/AF wings in November 1961 and flown the Mirage IIICJ from April 1964, he was killed over Egypt on June 5, 1967 while flying Shahak 04. It is believed that his jet was downed by "Atoll" AAMs fired from the MiG-21FL of Nabil Shoukry.

down the lead Shahak. Neuman was flying as a wingman.

At around the same time as this action was taking place, four Shahak pilots from No. 117 Sqn found themselves dogfighting a similar number of SyAAF MiG-21s. The quartet of IDF/AF aircraft had actually taken off from Ramat David as two separate CAP formations at 1250 hrs and 1258 hrs, respectively. Subsequently ordered to join up, the Shahaks were vectored onto enemy aircraft over Syria. Israeli IDF/AF GCI had attempted to place the fighters in a perfect position directly behind the MiG-21s, but by the time the controller called "targets at one mile, 12 o'clock", the SyAAF aircraft were actually sat just 600 metres *behind* the Shahaks! This grave directional error was the result of either poor IDF/AF GCI radar resolution or superior Syrian fighter control.

Quickly realising that his opponents clearly had the upper hand, Uri Gil in the No 4 jet broke hard into the closest MiG-21 without waiting to receive such an order from his leader. The "Fishbed" pilot pulled up into a zoom climb, with Gil following, but he was unable to close on the Syrian fighter due to the MiG-21's clear superiority over the Mirage IIICJ in a vertical fight. The Soviet aircraft also dived faster than its French counterpart, so shortly after the Shahak reached the apex of its zoom climb and fell away first in a dive, the MiG-21 quickly caught it up. The rival fighters plunged earthward literally back-to-back, a mere 20 metres apart, allowing both pilots time to closely examine one another – Gil subsequently reported that his opponent was inexplicably wearing a "brown leather helmet"!

As the Shahak pilot recovered from his dive, he saw that the MiG-21 had crept several hundred metres ahead of him. Grasping his opportunity, Gil opened fire and hit the SyAAF in the cockpit area. The "Fishbed" hit the ground moments later, its pilot having failed to eject.

A further ten pairs of Shahaks from No. 117 Sqn departed Ramat David on CAPs between 1306 hrs and 1719 hrs, and most of them flew eventless racetrack patterns over the Israeli/Syrian border. The exceptions were two jets that took-off at 1430 hrs and downed a Lebanese Hunter and a CAP pair that were scrambled at 1515 hrs. Leading this formation was squadron CO Amichai Shamueli, with Meir Shahar as his wingman. They too were vectored several times to engage enemy aircraft, but each intercept proved to be fruitless. Nearing the end of their CAP, the Shahak pilots were ordered to strafe an airfield in Damascus. This request probably arose because of an aborted attack on the same base by No. 101 Sqn. The Shahaks headed towards Damascus from their CAP position, the pair heading for the target at an altitude in excess of 20,000ft. Their plan was to attack the airfield in a steep diving pass, strafing along the runway's axis before turning for home. Shamueli explained what happened next:

I think that this action was unnecessary. The moment we came in, we noticed a tremendous amount of AAA in response to our strafing attack. I flew very fast – more than 500 knots – and very low, and as I neared the end of my strafing run I banked left and looked for my wingman, but he wasn't there. Suddenly I felt a tremendous kick in my backside. I pulled the control column with all my might and saw the silhouette of my aircraft pass by on the ground below me. The fire warning and hydraulic system 1 warning lights illuminated in the cockpit, the engine's RPM dropped and the aircraft slowed. It was at this point that I actually saw grass – I was that close to crashing. Then the fighter stabilised, and although it was flying really slowly, it was climbing, nevertheless.

I raised Reuven Harel (leader of the CAP pair that had departed Ramat David at 1528 hrs) on the radio, reported my situation and asked him to make a radio call for Meir Shachar (who had been shot down and killed over the airfield – author). They quickly joined me and reported that my aircraft was on fire. However, the engine continued to generate 75 percent thrust, and although the hydraulic system 2 warning light was now

This superb gunsight camera view was taken by a No. 119 Sqn Shahak pilot during his strafing attack on the SyAAF's T-4 base on June 5, 1967. The fighter's target is the MiG-15UTI parked in the distance behind the covered MiG-21FL that is still sat in the open on the airfield hours after the first Six Day War strikes had been flown.

No. 117 Sqn pilot Uri Gil was credited with downing an SyAAF MiG-21 while flying Shahak 70 on June 5, 1967. Squadronmate Uri Liss photographed the aircraft the following month adorned with two kill markings – both Syrian MiG-21s, with the second of Shahak 70's victories being credited to Ehud Henkin on June 9, 1967.

also on, I thought that this might be a false warning as the aircraft remained responsive to my control inputs. As I reached 8,000-9,000ft, my escorts again told me that I was on fire, and moments later the control column froze and I ejected.

The loss of both Shahaks was officially attributed to Syrian AAA fire by the IDF/AF, although its Intelligence section noted that a Syrian MiG-21 had intercepted the Israeli jets and shot them down.

That same afternoon, No. 119 Sqn sent a four-aircraft formation to attack the base known as T-4, which was located to the northeast of the Syrian capital. Using the call-sign "Fence", the aircraft had departed Tel Nof at 1514 hrs. Identified as "Fence 2", Giora Romm sighted "two MiGs, '12 o'clock high'" during his bombing run. The Shahak pilots pressed on with their attack nevertheless, dropping their ordnance and then coming back around again so as to make a series of strafing passes. No MiG-21s were seen during the first run, but during the second pass future ace Asher Snir ("Fence 4") spotted one of the enemy fighters. Jettisoning his external fuel tanks, he positioned his fighter directly behind the MiG-21 and opened fire. It was only after he had wasted two bursts that Snir noticed that his Shahak was "skidding", thus making it impossible for him to fire straight. By then the MiG-21 was "sandwiched" between "Fences 3 and 4". Snir corrected his aim, did his best to steady his jet and opened fire. This time the MiG-21 was engulfed in flames and crashed.

Moments later the remaining "Fishbed" targeted "Fence 3" with an AAM that failed to guide and a burst of cannon fire that missed. Romm quickly closed in on the MiG-21 and shot it down too.

On June 5 only six MiG-21 versus Mirage IIICJ engagements had generated kill claims resulting in an exchange ratio of two-to-one. Officially, Shahak units were credited with nine "Fishbed" kills for the loss of four French fighters and two pilots killed. Post-war, IDF/AF Intelligence reported that 24 MiG-21s crashed on this date – 17 Egyptian and seven Syrian. No fewer than 12 of these losses were attributed to either "friendly fire" or fuel starvation.

Although the aerial clashes between supersonic fighters on Day One of the war proved just how superior the Mirage IIICJ in Israeli hands was over the Arab MiG-21 force, the most important missions flown by the French aircraft on June 5 were the various air base attacks. IDF/AF Intelligence reported the destruction of 102 MiG-21s on the ground that day – 71 Egyptian, 25 Syrian and six Iraqi. Overall, Israeli pilots claimed 126 MiG-21s destroyed on June 5, this figure representing 65 percent of the IDF/AF's pre-war Arab order of battle evaluation of 194 "Fishbeds". In return, Israeli Shahak losses totalled just four aircraft. Yet despite the devastating nature of the airfield attacks on Day One, the EAF's fighter force in particular remained a powerful opponent. Indeed, the bulk of the MiG-21s destroyed had been sitting on the ground, which in turn meant that the Egyptians and the Syrians had only suffered minimal, and bearable, losses to their pilot cadre.

Between Day Two and Day Six of the war, Arab fighters were forced to operate in airspace dominated by marauding Shahaks. Pilots of the latter aircraft confidently flew both air-to-air and air-to-ground missions, the former being covered by Shahak CAP and QRA formations. The three fighter units were primarily providing close air support for IDF troops when tasked with flying air-to-ground missions, although they also occasionally performed air superiority missions such as airfield attack and the suppression of enemy air defences. Shahak air-to-air missions were flown in pairs, while four-aircraft formations undertook air-to-ground missions so as to enhance their offensive punch and improve mutual defence.

Although wary of Israeli fighters, Egyptian and Algerian MiG-21 squadrons continued to operate in a similar manner to their Shahak counterparts throughout the war. Syrian units, however, undertook only a handful of patrols as the SyAAF tried to conserve its remaining air power. Consequently, Syrian troops on the Golan Heights were heavily attacked by the IDF/AF, shattering their valiant defence. The continuous dawn to dusk Shahak CAP flown over the SyAAF's main MiG-21 base at Dmer from Day Two through to Day Six may have also had something to do with the Syrian fighter force's reluctance to fight!

Iraqi MiG-21 operations were limited to defensive CAPs flown to protect H-3 in the west of the country, as it was the only forward IrAF base within range of Israeli combat aircraft. In fact the first MiG-21 versus Mirage engagement of Day Two took place over H-3 when the IDF/AF mounted three attack missions aimed at preventing the IrAF from participating in the conflict. The Iraqis were well prepared for such an air raid, with IDF/AF aircraft having to fight IrAF fighters on all three missions. Only the second of these events saw Mirage IIICJs clash with MiG-21s, however.

The aircraft involved in this mission had departed Ramat David at 0631 hrs (four Vautours) and 0633 hrs (two escorting Shahaks from No. 117 Sqn) on the morning of June 6. Although the initial air-to-air action over H-3 had involved Shahaks and Vautours fighting Hunters, minutes after the disengagement order was given, the escort leader, future ace Yehuda Koren, saw a MiG-21 attacking a Vautour – he had already downed one of the Hunters. Koren rushed to the aircraft's aid, as Vautour pilot Beni Zohar recalled:

I had just finished my strafing pass when the Vautour leader ordered us to disengage. It was at this point that I saw a MiG-21 heading straight towards me in a beautiful dive as part of a scissors manoeuvre, and I broke sharply for the ground. He in turn climbed steeply in preparation for another diving attack on my aircraft. It was at this point that I managed to radio my leader, telling him that I couldn't disengage, and that I was in a "scissors" fight with a MiG-21. Koren then told me over the radio "Leave him, leave him. He is mine!" I found this rather funny because I wasn't actually chasing him. Indeed, I was only trying to defend myself.

Koren took full advantage of the MiG-21 pulling up. I was very, very close to the IrAF fighter when the Shahak's cannon fired. Almost instantly the MiG-21 froze in the air, burst into flames and spun away. Koren's action was so skilful – it was beautiful, sharp, smooth and simple. This was also the only time that I saw an air-to-air kill.

The only MiG-21 versus Mirage IIICJ engagement over Sinai on Day Two saw Shahaks from Nos. 101 and 119 Sqns intercept a pair of MiG-21FLs. Two QRA pairs had scrambled on CAPs, the No. 101 Sqn jets taking off from Hatzor at 0953 hrs and the Shahaks from No. 119 Sqn departing Tel Nof seven minutes later. Both pairs carried out typical wartime CAPs, which consisted in the main of flying a racetrack pattern with the occasional vector to intercept unidentified targets – some turned out to be Israeli jets returning from missions, while others were fleeing enemy aircraft that were too far away to be intercepted.

The No. 101 Sqn fighters were approaching their fuel limits when GCI vectored them onto enemy aircraft over northwest Sinai. The controller ordered the Shahak pilots to turn to the right, but Guri Palter in the lead jet suffered radio failure and did not change course. His wingman, Giora Furman, managed to get into position right behind one of the contacts, which turned out to be an EAF MiG-21. Opening fire from 300 metres, the enemy jet was hit a number of times and the Egyptian pilot ejected. By then Palter had also turned, but the pair had to disengage because their fuel state was now dangerously low. The remaining MiG-21 pilot seized his chance and positioned his jet 2,500 metres directly behind Palter's Shahak.

The No. 119 Sqn CAP pair had also been vectored against the "Fishbeds", and wingman Ithamar Neuner was the first to spot the MiG-21 chasing Palter. With the

Yehuda Koren strikes a casual pose in front of the No. 117 Sqn building at Ramat David. Having earned his IDF/AF wings in March 1962, he flew the Shahak from April 1965 until 1982. During that time Koren claimed 10.5 aerial victories. He retired with the rank of colonel.

EAF pilot intent on the Shahak in front of him, Neuner succeeded in getting onto the tail of the enemy fighter without being seen and he launched a Shafrir. Predictably, the AAM failed to guide, as did the second one that he fired. Alerted to the danger, the MiG-21 pilot immediately broke off his attack and turned for home. Diving towards the ground, the "Fishbed" was chased by Neuner until he got to within cannon range. His first burst missed, but his second found its mark. The MiG-21 slowed dramatically and Neuner overshot his prey. While turning around to get back into position to finish the fighter off, his leader, Uri Ye'ari, came in and shot the "Fishbed" down!

The only recorded MiG-21 versus Mirage IIICJ engagement of Day Three involved a pair of Shahaks returning from Iraq. Earlier that day, three IAF jets (two Vautours and a Shahak from No. 117 Sqn) had been lost over H-3 to AAA and IrAF Hunters. No. 117 Sqn pilots Ezra "Baban" Dotan (a future ace) and David Porat had been the leader and sub-leader of the Shahak escort that had initially departed Ramat David for H-3 at 1023 hrs. Having claimed one of two Hunters downed during the course of this ill-fated mission, Dotan and his wingman had returned to base, refuelled and rearmed, and then sortied from Ramat David at 1401 hrs to help in the search for the missing pilots. David Porat explains what happened next:

We realised during the debrief of the H-3 attack mission that nobody had seen any of the missing aircraft actually crash, so it was decided to return to the target area and search for the lost jets. I flew with "Baban" along the same route, but we saw nothing. Once over H-3 we flew a single strafing pass and then turned for home. On our way back we strafed elements of the Iraqi expeditionary force prior to climbing up to altitude for the final leg of the flight to Ramat David.

As we flew over Jabel Druz and spotted the Sea of Galilee as a tiny dot off to the west, I suddenly saw little puffs of smoke near "Baban". As I called him on the radio and told him to watch out for AAA, I realised that it wasn't possible for flak to reach such a high altitude (37,000ft). As I looked behind the Shahak I was alarmed to see an AAM heading for it. I told "Baban" to "break" and the missile exploded nearby. Two MiG-21s followed the AAM, and at exactly the same moment I saw two Shahaks zooming up towards us as well. Apparently our GCI tracked us returning from H-3, as well as two SyAAF MiG-21s that had taken off from Dmer. Once they had detected the Syrian jets, GCI forgot all about us, and figured that all four aircraft were MiG-21s! They had scrambled Yehuda Koren and his wingman to intercept what they thought were two Syrian pairs regrouping into one four-ship formation. With "Baban's" jet badly damaged, Koren told us to "Go home. I will engage the MiGs".

Dotan broke hard into the SyAAF jets despite the damage to his Shahak, thus evading the pursuing MiG-21PFs that had fired "Atolls" at the high-flying IDF/AF aircraft. Fortunately for Dotan, only one of the AAMs had exploded near his aircraft. By turning into his opponents, he was sticking to his personal mantra – "successful air combat is all about seeing and deceiving". Now knowing exactly where his foes were, Dotan had to deceive them into thinking that the Shahak still posed a threat to them.

This photograph of Ezra Dotan's Shahak 29 was taken immediately after it had landed at Megiddo on June 7, 1967 following a near miss by an "Atoll" fired from a SyAAF MiG-21. The Israeli fighter's skilful, and lucky, pilot can be seen standing by the right wingtip, looking at the damage inflicted to the jet's empennage. A forklift had to be used to pull the fighter's Atar turbojet from the fuselage. Once a replacement had been hastily installed, Dotan ferried Shahak 29 from Megiddo to Ramat David on the evening of June 8. The re-engined fighter duly flew six more missions during the final two days of the war.

Face-to-face with the lead MiG-21, Dotan gambled on the Syrian pilot performing a routine crossover manoeuvre and then instigating a climbing turn, which he duly did. Anxious to disengage and nurse his damaged fighter home, Dotan dived. However, the MiG-21 returned, so the Israeli pilot was again forced into deceiving his foe by pointing his nose directly at him. The "Fishbed" was much faster than the damaged Shahak, and it quickly flashed by him. This time Dotan opted for a much steeper dive down to 7,000ft, which shook the MiG-21 off. Such a manoeuvre jeopardised his chances of making a successful landing, however, as the Shahak's badly damaged engine had quit during the dive. Showing superior airmanship, Dotan stretched the delta fighter's glide just far enough so that he could land at the general aviation airfield at Megiddo, touching down at 230 knots, but still managing to stop the Shahak on the runway without further damaging the precious fighter.

Four Shahak pairs intercepted enemy aircraft over north Sinai during the afternoon of June 8, with three of them engaging MiG-21s. First to fight was No. 119 Sqn's "Gutter" section, which had departed Tel Nof at 1505 hrs. Flying "Gutter 2" was Menachem Shmul:

We were scrambled after more than two hours of QRA, sitting in our cockpits in the hot afternoon sun. Having vectored us south, GCI then told us to head for Romani, some 80-90 miles away, after receiving reports that Il-28s and MiGs were attacking our troops. Initially, we flew with full dry power, but then we switched to full afterburner. As we flew over Bardawil, we were ordered to descend, and when we reached 5,000ft I saw an Il-28 flying low over the sea in a northeasterly direction. I reported the sighting to my leader, Ya'acov Agassi, and then turned towards the bomber. Given permission to shoot it down, I closed to 1,000-1,200 metres, at which point the Il-28's rear gunner started firing at me. I opened fire at a distance of 800 metres in an attempt to silence the gunner, but he didn't stop firing. Closing to 500 metres, I fired a rather long burst that hit the Il-28 in the empennage, causing some of its fuel tanks to explode. The bomber flew on like a torch towards the beach, crashing on land and exploding 30 seconds later.

We then headed south before turning west once again. After a minute or so Agassi saw some MiG-21s heading in the opposite direction to us – they passed directly underneath us. We quickly turned around, after which I levelled my wings prior to jettisoning my external fuel tanks. It was at this point that I spotted another MiG-21 following my leader. He was below me, so I turned towards him, climbed steeply so as to gain even more of a height advantage and then converted this into speed when I dived onto his tail. Opening fire with a short burst, I saw cannon rounds crashing into him. The MiG-21 exploded in a fireball, and the resulting shock wave rocked my Shahak so violently that I was sure that my aircraft had been damaged. I reported this, and my leader ordered me to disengage. A short while later we regrouped and returned to base. Post-flight examination revealed minor damage near the engine intakes of my fighter, caused by small fragments of disintegrating MiG-21.

Shmul's after action report matches the recollections of Inshas-based MiG-21 pilot Nabil Shoukry, who was involved in a ground attack mission east of the Suez Canal when the Shahaks appeaared:

For my second sortie of the day, my jet was solely equipped with two of those awful ground-attack rocket pods that we were using against Israeli tanks in north Sinai. After we had flown over the Suez Canal we spotted two Mirages heading towards us from the left, so I put the afterburner on, jettisoned the belly tank and saw that they were going

The badly damaged Atar 09B-3 engine that was removed from Ezra Dotan's Shahak. As this photograph clearly shows, the exhaust section had borne the brunt of the explosion when the "Atoll" detonated near the tail of the Israeli jet.

Both Arab MiG-21 pilots and their Israeli Mirage IIICJ counterparts used fighter formations that were universally employed throughout the world. The most common were the slightly modified "fluid four" and single file "trail" formations. The former, which was more popular amongst Shahak pilots, was utilised prior to combat as it maximised situational awareness and mutual defence at the expense of ease of manoeuvrability – the latter proved to be less important in the high-speed rear hemisphere interceptions that were commonplace in the Middle East throughout the 1960s. The distances between the aircraft in the "fluid four" were dependent on weather conditions and altitude. The single file formation was seen in use by both sides during CAPs and at the start of combat between opposing fighters. Shahak and SyAAF MiG-21 section leaders and their wingmen would readily split up depending on how their engagement progressed. EAF "Fishbed" pilots endeavoured to remain together at all times, however, with Shahak pilots reporting gaps of as little as 50 metres between leaders and their wingmen. Again, the distances between the leader and his wingman, as well as between pairs of fighters, varied according to weather conditions and altitude. The single file formation was not limited to two pairs, and on many occasions MiG-21 pilots entered combat in a "train" of four to eight pairs, all flying in single file formation. Unlike in World War II, neither formation boasted a "prime shooter". Instead, whoever spotted the enemy first would invariably lead the attack.

to attack. I told my leader "There's a Mirage behind you". He reversed, but at that moment his MiG-21 exploded after being hit by cannon fire. The Mirage then headed for el-Arish. I put the nose down and selected maximum afterburner, but the rocket-pods created a lot of drag. I reached the same altitude as the Mirage and got to within a mile of it, but I had no way of closing because it was accelerating. I started firing unguided rockets at him from each pod, but they fell well short.

MiG-21 versus Mirage IIICJ action during the first three days of the war mostly took the form of classic two-versus-two engagements. And even when the number of jets involved exceeded four, the action usually broke up into individual duels within the overall melee. For example, the June 5 clashes over Abu Sueir saw two Shahak pilots credited with four kills between them following a series of duels during the airfield strike, rather than during one continuous action against four or more enemy aircraft.

Multi-bogey engagements commenced, however, on the afternoon of Day Four over northwest Sinai following a resurgence in Egyptian air activity. A multi-bogey fight essentially saw jets from both sides fighting it out in a single action, rather than aircraft pairing off for a series of individual duels. Egyptian fighter pilots tended to fight in "rigid" pairs, with the wingman following his leader at all times, resisting the opportunity to break off and hunt down his own prey. The IDF/AF, therefore, treated a two-versus-four action as a typical engagement, but classified a dogfight with more participants as a multi-bogey clash.

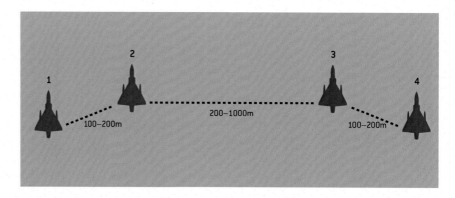

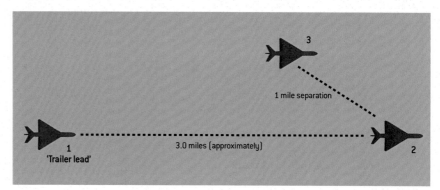

Although the latter provided Shahak pilots with more kill opportunities, high levels of situational awareness were also required. Focusing attention on a single target during a multi-bogey engagement left the pilot exposed to possible attack from other enemy aircraft. The principal characteristics of a successful multi-bogey engagement were fast, decisive manoeuvres, the ability to quickly switch from one target to another and knowing when to alter your mindset from hunter to hunted. All had to be achieved within split seconds.

When GCI vectored a CAP off station to intercept a target, a QRA pair was also scrambled to fill the CAP vacuum. The drawback of this strategy was that Shahak pilots were sometimes vectored to engage contacts towards the end of their allotted time on CAP, by which point their fuel state was already too low for prolonged air combat – especially against multiple bogeys. This was precisely what happened to the No. 101 Sqn CAP that departed Hatzor at 1542 hrs on June 8. Yosef Arazi and Maoz Poraz had been on their CAP station for 30+ minutes when GCI issued them with a vector to engage. The Shahak pilots were down to 1,200 litres of fuel – less than half of their internal fuel load – by the time they spotted EAF jets over northwest Sinai.

Leader Arazi intercepted a lone MiG-21 that he saw attacking IDF troops, and moments later four more "Fishbeds" and a similar number of MiG-17s entered the fray. Arazi chased after a MiG-21 but had to break off his attack when a second EAF fighter launched air-to-ground rockets at him. The Shahaks separated moments later, with both Poraz and Arazi turning their attention to two MiG-17s. Again Arazi was forced to take evasive action when he became embroiled in a scissors manoeuvre with a MiG-21 that soon overtook him. While still fighting the "Fishbed", he suddenly saw another MiG-21 that simply flew across his nose. Arazi opened fire but excitement got the better of him and his aim was poor. Forcing himself to calm down, he fired a longer burst until the MiG-21 exploded. No ejection was observed. The Shahak leader then saw another MiG-21 flying 600 metres away at a high deflection angle – far from ideal, but in a multi-bogey engagement such a fleeting opportunity had to be

Shahak 73 rotates from the runway at Hatzor, its auxiliary air intake doors open. The latter were essential if the engine was to receive the required volume of air needed to generate the higher thrust necessary for take-off. This aircraft was lost in combat over Sinai on June 8, 1967.

seized. Arazi opened fire, missed and duly exhausted his ammunition. It was now time to disengage. Arazi landed at a forward airfield with less than 100 litres of fuel remaining in the tanks of his Shahak. His wingman was not so lucky, Poraz having to eject from his fuel-starved Shahak.

The final Day Four MiG-21 versus Mirage IIICJ engagement also involved a No. 101 Sqn CAP that took off from Hatzor at 1730 hrs on a dusk patrol. The EAF fighters were encountered over northwest Sinai, but the results of the action were inconclusive.

The last Six Day War clash between Arab and Israeli fighters took place during the afternoon of June 9 over the SyAAF MiG-21 base at Dmer. As previously mentioned, No. 117 Sqn Shahaks had maintained daylight CAPs over the airfield from Day One of the conflict, and these had been generally successful. By the last day of the war activity in Sinai had declined following the IDF occupation, so the Israelis mounted a late offensive in the Golan Heights. This may have prompted a Syrian attempt to launch fighters from Dmer.

Ehud Henkin was the wingman for a QRA pair scrambled from Ramat David at 1227 hrs to fly a routine CAP over the SyAAF base. Once on station they were quickly vectored onto a Syrian MiG-21, which Henkin shot down. No. 117 Sqn records indicate that the kill was achieved directly over Dmer, but the official IDF/AF victory certificate awarded to Henkin states that the action took place over T-4, which was another Syrian MiG-21 base well to the north of Dmer.

The latter was definitely the scene of the final Six Day War MiG-21 versus Mirage engagement, however. No. 117 Sqn pilots Yehuda Koren and Avi Oren had been scrambled from Ramat David at 1720 hrs on June 10, some five-and-a-half hours after the ceasefire between Israel and the Arab nations had come into effect. Aerial activity remained tense, nevertheless, and as the Shahaks flew CAP over the Golan Heights protecting IDF/AF helicopters airlifting Israeli troops into forward positions, GCI vectored the pair to intercept SyAAF MiG-21s that had attacked an IDF/AF Piper Cub observation aircraft. The "Fishbeds" were tracked flying back to Dmer, with the Shahaks in pursuit. Visual contact was achieved at 20,000ft over the base when Oren spotted one of the MiG-21s hastily taxiing back into its shelter.

An American tourist poses beside the tail and drop tank of an EAF MiG-21FL a few weeks after it was shot down in northern Sinai during the Six Day War.

ANALYSIS AND STATISTICS

Israeli Mirage IIICJs engaged Arab MiG-21s at least 25 times between July 19, 1964 and June 10, 1967. Some of these encounters were only fleeting, while others evolved into fully blown air combat. Victories were claimed or credited during 17 of these engagements. As these numbers clearly show, the probability of Mirage IIICJ or MiG-21 pilots participating in aerial combat was slim prior to the Six Day War, and only marginally better during the more intensive wartime operations in early June 1967.

According to available IDF/AF data, Shahak pilots flew 1,077 sorties and fought MiG-21s on 16 occasions during the Six Day War. These engagements took place during the course of 22 Shahak missions (in a few combats more than one Shahak formation participated in the clash) totalling 55 sorties. Based on these statistics, Shahak pilots saw a MiG-21 in the air in only 5.1 percent of the sorties flown during the conflict! Ten of the sixteen engagements (37 sorties in total) ended in "Fishbed" kills, so the probability of a Shahak pilot participating in a successful air combat was only 3.4 percent. As these figures clearly show, participation in a successful air combat was no guarantee that an individual pilot would achieve a kill credit. In fact only 13 of the 37 sorties that resulted in a victory generated individual kill credits. To summarise, Shahak pilots participating in Six Day War missions encountered MiG-21s in just 5.1 percent of the sorties flown, this figure dropping to 3.4 percent for those that enjoyed success and just 1.2 percent for pilots credited with a kill.

Arab MiG-21 data for the conflict is unavailable, but it is fair to assume that "Fishbed" pilots probably engaged Mirage IIICJs at much the same rate. However, the probability of them achieving a kill was significantly lower simply because few Shahak victories were credited to MiG-21s. Indeed, the Mirage IIICJ versus "Fishbed"

This IDF/AF battle damage assessment photograph of Dmer air base, in Syria, was taken on the afternoon of June 5, 1967. To the left of the image, five bomb craters and one near miss can just be seen along the length of runway 24. Two more bomb craters have been left by attacking Israeli aircraft just to the left of the parallel taxiway. The five black "stains" on the aprons to the right of the taxiway and near the runway threshold are almost certainly burnt-out MiG-21s that were destroyed during strafing attacks. With no intact "Fishbeds" visible in this view, it is reasonable to believe that the remaining MiG-21s at Dmer were quickly hidden within the shelters visible in the bottom right hand corner of this photograph. The final Six Day War MiG-21 versus Mirage IIICJ encounter ended when a "Fishbed" was seen to hastily taxi into one of these shelters on June 10, 1967.

air-to-air kill ratio was 8-to-80 during pre-Six Day War clashes and 15-to-5 during the Six Day War itself. The overall ratio was 5-to-1. Since this data is based on IDF/AF victories and losses only, the 5-to-1 ratio should be treated as a maximum figure. It is somewhat distorted, however, as the statistics fail to take into account overall air superiority enjoyed by the IDF/AF after June 5, 1967. Simply put, Israeli Shahaks were much more effective in the Six Day War than Arab MiG-21s.

The IDF/AF's post-war analysis of the air combats that had been fought credited the Shahak with 13 confirmed MiG-21 kills. Of these, 12 were awarded to pilots and the 13th was an aircraft that crashed before No. 101 Sqn pilot Dan Sever could open fire – he later received credit for its demise. Two additional aerial victory credits were awarded after the conflict, the first of these being to No. 119 Sqn pilot Eitan Karmi for a Day One kill over Abu Sueir, and the second to No. 117 Sqn's Yehuda Koren for a Day Two kill over H-3. Even with these additional victories there is still a substantial gap between the initial IDF/AF Six Day War MiG-21 kill credits figure of 15 (13 to Shahaks and two to other fighter types) and an official statement released shortly after the war that claimed 37 MiG-21s (29 Egyptian and eight Syrian) had been "destroyed in the air" during the conflict!

The IDF/AF admitted the loss of ten Shahaks in combat during the same period – one prior to the Six Day War and nine during the conflict itself. All were lost in the air. Five of these were probably downed during engagements with MiG-21s. The Israelis claimed to have destroyed 156 MiG-21s in 1966-67, 100 of them Egyptian (all during the Six Day War), 41 Syrian (including eight prior to the Six Day War) and 15 Iraqi (again all during the Six Day War). Based on these numbers, the overall

No. 101 Sqn's Shahak 09 flew 18 sorties between June 5 and 10, 1967 — eight QRA scrambles/offensive CAPs, six air support missions and four air superiority missions. The latter took the form of two air base strikes, one radar attack mission and an SA-2 missile battery attack. The Shahak encountered an Arab fighter in the air just once during the Six Day War when Amos Amir fought an EAF MiG-19 on June 7 whilst flying an air support mission. Two of the four Shahaks that participated in this action with the Egyptian MiG-19s were credited with kills, including Shahak 09.

MiG-21 v Mirage IIICJ Engagements July 1964–June 1967

Date	Nation	Shahak Squadron	MiG losses	Shahak losses
July 19, 1964	Egypt	119	-	-
November 14, 1964	Syria	101	-	-
July 14, 1966	Syria	101	1	-
August 15, 1966	Syria	117	1	-
April 7, 1967	Syria	101	2	-
April 7, 1967	Syria	117	-	-
April 7, 1967	Syria	119	1	-
April 7, 1967	Syria	117/101	3	-
May 26, 1967	Egypt	101/119	-	-
June 5, 1967	Egypt	101	1	-
June 5, 1967	Egypt	119	-	-
June 5, 1967	Egypt	117/119	4	-
June 5, 1967	Syria	117	1	1
June 5, 1967	Egypt	101	-	1
June 5, 1967	Syria	117	1	-
June 5, 1967	Syria	119	2	-
June 5, 1967	Syria	117	-	2
June 6, 1967	Iraq	117	1	-
June 6, 1967	Egypt	101/119	2	-
June 7, 1967	Syria	117	-	-
June 8, 1967	Egypt	119	1	-
June 8, 1967	Egypt	101	1	1
June 8, 1967	Egypt	101	-	-
June 9, 1967	Syria	117	1	-
June 10, 1967	Syria	117	-	-

Air base missions on June 5, 1967 produced substantially more claims for MiG-21s destroyed than air-to-air action throughout the entire Six Day War. Indeed, photographs of Arab "Fishbeds" being strafed on the ground – or, as in this case, post-mission images of burnt out EAF fighters – came to symbolise the IDF/AF's victory in the conflict more than gunsight camera frames showing aerial kills.

MiG-21-to-Mirage IIICJ combat loss ratio was 16-to-1. However, Shahaks were not responsible for all of these MiG-21 combat losses, and vice versa. IDF/AF data states that 111 MiG-21s were destroyed on the ground and 45 shot down – only 23 of the latter fell to Shahaks.

Air-to-air weapons available to Middle Eastern Mach 2 pilots during this period were cannon and AAMs – the EAF also used unguided air-to-ground rockets on at least two occasions. The "Fishbed's" primary air-to-air weapon was the "Atoll" infrared-homing AAM. Indeed, it was the MiG-21FL's only weapon! The MiG-21F-13 also had a single 30mm cannon which was limited to just 30 rounds. Theoretically, the Shahak was better armed with air-to-air weaponry. This included the Matra R 530 Yahalom semi-active radar-homing AAM, the Rafael Shafrir infrared-homing AAM and two 30mm DEFA 552 cannon, with 250 rounds. However, the Yahalom was only available to a handful of QRA jets, and Shahaks routinely flew with only a single Shafrir. As has been repeatedly mentioned in this volume, both weapons were chronically unreliable in any case. By default, therefore, the cannon became the Shahak's principal air-to-air weapon.

No fewer than 22 of the 23 MiG-21 kills credited to Shahak pilots in 1966-67 were claimed with cannon – the other victory was a "no weapon" manoeuvre kill. Conversely, three of the five Shahaks lost to MiG-21s during the same period fell to "Atoll" AAMs. The remaining two were again "no weapon" kills – one jet was downed by the debris from an exploding MiG-21 and the other ran out of fuel. The fact that the Shahak boasted two cannon and adequate ammunition gave the jet a real advantage over the MiG-21 during the 1960s, as AAM technology was still then in its infancy.

The MiG-21 and Mirage IIICJ were perhaps the most closely matched Mach 2 fighters to have ever gone head-to-head in combat. Nevertheless, the French machine emerged the clear victor with an air-to-air kills-to-losses ratio of 6-to-1, and a total combat losses ratio of 16-to-1 thanks to the Shahak's superiority in air-to-air weaponry, the knowledge its pilot had of the MiG-21 and sound IDF/AF tactics.

AFTERMATH

Simple and uncharismatic, IDF/AF commander-in-chief Moti Hod was always in the shadow of his predecessor, the temperamental and charismatic Ezer Weizman. The latter had led the IDF/AF from 1958 until 1966, when Hod took over, and he then served as IDF Chief of the General Staff Branch until 1969. Yet there can be little doubt that the two officers with opposing personalities made immense contributions in their own special way to the IDF/AF's greatest victory – the Six Day War. Hod wrote in 1972:

> The Six Day War was preceded by lengthy preparations and training. Prewar, the IDF/AF trained, developed tactics and prepared for the day when its full abilities and capabilities would be needed. These preparations instilled self-confidence and a sense of power among IDF/AF service personnel and faith among commanders that when the day came, they would exploit their full potential in the air and on the ground to decisively defeat the enemy. Such a defeat would secure air superiority and enable the IDF forces to rapidly advance without interference from the air – and with the active cooperation of the IDF/AF. The Six Day War victory was the result of many reasons, but the principal ingredients were:
>
> a) Simple planning.
> b) An almost perfect match between planning and operations.
> c) IDF/AF pilots utilising their flying skills to precisely execute their mission tasking.
> d) Central control.
> e) Intelligence.

In many ways this seemingly simplistic overview accurately sums up both how the Six Day War was won in general and how the numerically superior MiG-21 force was

Israeli pilots were well aware of the MiG-21's strengths and weaknesses thanks to this ex-Iraqi MiG-21F-13, which was appropriately renumbered 007. Photographed in Israel following its return from the USA, where it was evaluated between January and April 1968, the jet was probably responsible not only for the Shahak's superiority over Arab MiG-21s but also for the improvement in the US air-to-air kills-to-losses ratio over Vietnam. The latter went from 2-to-1 (USAF) and 3-to-1 (US Navy) in 1968 to 3-to-1 (USAF) and 8-to-1 (US Navy) in 1972.

decimated by the three Mirage IIICJ squadrons in particular. Having managed to achieve an almost perfect match between prewar training and real combat, the IDF/AF quickly had the upper hand in the short conflict that was fought across three very different fronts topographically – the Sinai Desert, the hilly terrain of the West Bank and the flat volcanic plain of the Golan Heights.

The conflict between the Arab nations and Israel continued in the years that followed the Six Day War, but MiG-21s and Mirage IIICJs fought each other in combat only until 1974. More modern fighters then began to prevail. What was the long-term impact of the duels between the Soviet and French interceptors in later

The surviving Shahaks soldiered on in IDF/AF service into the early 1980s, when a number of them were sold to Argentina as attrition replacements following the 1982 Falklands War. One of the aircraft sent to South America was this machine, Shahak 59, which was the top scoring Mirage IIICJ of them all. Seen here shortly before it departed, the jet spent a number of years on display in front of a regional school in Argentina prior to being acquired by the IDF/AF Museum and shipped back to Israel.

Most Arab MiG-21s were camouflaged in the wake of the Six Day War, including this rather unusual EAF aircraft. Either rebuilt from undamaged parts after the June 1967 war or extensively modified in Egypt, the basic machine is a MiG-21PFM with the brake parachute fairing above the jet-pipe partially replaced or just left unpainted. The tailfin, however, is of the narrower type, characteristic of a MiG-21F-13 or MiG-21PF. There also seem to have been repairs or modifications made to the fighter's fuselage spine, while the canopy has been replaced too. Finally, the fighter's camouflage appears to be an early, perhaps experimental, version of the "Nile Valley" scheme developed in Egypt in the early 1970s.

conflicts in the region? In respect to the Arab air forces, Egypt led the way with a programme of massive air base rebuilding and the creation of the Egyptian Air Defence Force (EADF) as an independent fourth military service. The latter was equipped with highly effective SAMs and AAA batteries, all controlled by an extensive radar network. Tasked primarily with defending the EAF's resurrected airfields, the EADF ensured that Egyptian bases would never again experience the levels of destruction meted out to them during the Six Day War. This in turn meant that there were many more MiG-21s available for air combat in future conflicts. And more Arab fighters aloft resulted in considerably higher kill claims by Shahak pilots between 1969 and 1974.

In the air, the Arab air forces replaced their horrendous Six Day War MiG-21 losses with newer variants of the "Fishbed". Aircraft such as the MiG-21PFM and MiG-21MF were supplied in large quantities, and both types were better armed and boasted improved radar in an attempt to give them more of a multi-role capability. Conversely, the Israeli Mirage IIICJ fleet effectively went the opposite way during the same period – from multi-role to single mission. A French arms embargo and increased US support were the initial driving forces behind this change. The former rendered the surviving Mirage IIICJs far too valuable to sacrifice in ground attack missions, while the urgent introduction of the far more capable F-4E Phantom II into IDF/AF service from 1969 meant that the Shahak force could be exclusively assigned to the air defence role.

In later years, a number of former Arab MiG-21 and Israeli Mirage IIICJ pilots progressed through the ranks to occupy senior positions within their respective air forces. Indeed the current commander of the EAF, Air Marshal Magdy Galal Sharawi, flew the "Fishbed" for many years in the frontline. Likewise, his IDF/AF counterpart from 2004 to 2008, Maj Gen Eliezer Shkedy, was a Shahak pilot during the early stages of his military career. Even the first Israeli astronaut, Col Ilan Ramon, flew the Mirage IIICJ in the 1970s.

The IDF/AF retired the last of its Shahaks in 1982, but the "Fishbed", in Soviet-built MiG-21MF and MiG-21bis form, remains in frontline service with both the EAF and the SyAAF. The Egyptians also have a number of Chinese-built F-7s (improved MiG-21F-13s) on strength too.

FURTHER READING

BOOKS

Aloni, Shlomo, *Osprey Combat Aircraft 23 – Arab-Israeli Wars 1947–82*
   (Osprey Publishing, 2001)
Aloni, Shlomo, *Osprey Aircraft of the Aces 59 – Israeli Mirage and Nesher Aces*
   (Osprey Publishing, 2004)
Aloni, Shlomo, *101 – The First Fighter Squadron* (IsraDecal Publications, 2007)
Aloni, Shlomo, *Israeli Air Force Tayeset 119* (AirDOC, 2007)
Aloni, Shlomo, *The June 1967 Six Day War, Volume A – Operation* Focus
   (IsraDecal Publications, 2008)
Amir, Amos, *Fire in the Sky* (Pen & Sword, 2005)
Carlier, Claude and Luc Berger, *Dassault – 50 Years of Aeronautical Adventure*
   (editions du chene, 1996)
Cohen, Eliezer, *Israel's Best Defence* (Airlife, 1993)
Ginor, Isabella and Gideon Remez, *Foxbats Over Dimona* (Yale University Press, 2007)
Gordon, Yefim, Keith Dexter and Dmitriy Komissarov, *Mikoyan MiG-21*
   (Ian Allan Publishing, 2008)
Green, William and Gordon Swanborough, *The Complete Book of Fighters*
   (Salamander, 1994)
Gunston, Bill, *The Osprey Encyclopedia of Russian Aircraft 1875–1995*
   (Osprey Publishing, 1995)
Huertas Mafé, Salvador, *Dassault-Breguet Mirage III/5* (Osprey Publishing, 1990)
Mersky, Peter, *Israeli Fighter Aces* (Speciality Press, 1997)

Nicolle, David and Tom Cooper, *Osprey Combat Aircraft 44 – MiG-19 and MiG-21 Units in Combat* (Osprey Publishing, 2004)

Nordeen, Lon, *Fighters Over Israel* (Guild Publishing, 1991)

Nordeen, Lon and David Nicolle, *Phoenix Over The Nile* (Smithsonian Institution Press, 1996)

Norton, Bill, *Air War on the Edge* (Midland Publishing, 2004)

Spector, Iftach, *Loud and Clear* (Zenith Press, 2009)

Spick, Mike, *Fighter Pilot Tactics* (Patrick Stephens Ltd, 1983)

Spick, Mike, *Jet Fighter Performance – Korea to Vietnam* (Ian Allan Publishing, 1986)

Spick, Mike, *The Ace Factor – Air Combat and the Role of Situational Awareness* (Airlife Publishing, 1988)

Yonai, Ehud, *No Margin for Error* (Pantheon Books, 1993)

PERIODICALS

Aloni, Shlomo, *Shahaks over the Sinai – 101 Sqn, IDF/AF in the Six Day War* (Wings of Fame Volumes 16 and 17, 1999)

Aloni, Shlomo, *Best form of Defence? Attack! Hitting Abu Sueir during the Six Day War* (Air Enthusiast 123, 2006)

Aloni, Shlomo, *Six Days in June* (Aeroplane, June 2007)

INDEX

References to illustrations are shown in **bold**.